THEMATIC UNIT
Ancient Rome

Written by Mike Shepherd

Teacher Created Resources, Inc.
6421 Industry Way
Westminster, CA 92683
www.teachercreated.com
©*1995 Teacher Created Resources, Inc.*
Reprinted, 2006
Made in U.S.A.
ISBN-1-55734-596-1

Edited by
Barbara M. Wally

Illustrated by
Agi Palinay

Cover Art by
Agi Palinay

Table of Contents

Introduction

Roman civilization has made important and lasting contributions to the culture of our country and the entire world. Located in the middle of the Mediterranean Sea, Rome conquered and dominated this area and gave it a lasting peace for almost 1,000 years. In the process, Roman engineers made the first extensive use of paved roads, the arch, and modern plumbing. They gave us a standard for public buildings, some of which still remain standing in the 20th century. Our legal and political systems can be traced to Roman times. They also gave us a rich heritage of language. Latin is not a dead language: it lives in modern law, medicine, and other fields.

The first half of this unit gives a basic outline of Roman history from its origins through the decline and fall of the Roman Empire. The second half of the unit explores the daily life of Roman citizens and Rome's cultural heritage.

This thematic unit includes:

❏ **literature selections**—summary of *Ancient Rome*, an excellent "museum" book, with related lessons that cross the curriculum

❏ **language experience and writing ideas**—suggestions for a variety of creative writing experiences as well as activities across the curriculum

❏ **bulletin board ideas**—suggestions for student-created displays

❏ **curriculum connections**—in language arts, math, geography, history, and art

❏ **a bibliography**—suggestions for additional literature and nonfiction books on the theme

❏ **group projects**—to foster cooperative learning

❏ **culminating activities**—which require students to synthesize their learning to create a product or engage in an activity that can be shared with others

---

To keep this valuable resource intact so that it can be used year after year, you may wish to punch holes in the pages and store them in a three-ring binder.

Why a Balanced Approach?

The strength of a whole language approach is that it involves children in using all modes of communication—reading, writing, listening, illustrating, and doing. Communication skills are interconnected and integrated into lessons that emphasize the whole of language. Balancing this approach is our knowledge that every whole—including individual words—is composed of parts, and directed study of those parts can help a student to master the whole. Experience and research tell us that regular attention to phonics, other word attack skills, spelling, etc., develops reading mastery, thereby fulfilling the unity of the whole language experience. The child is thus led to read, write, spell, speak, and listen confidently in response to a literature experience introduced by the teacher. In these ways, language skills grow rapidly, stimulated by direct practice, involvement, and interest in the topic at hand.

Why Thematic Planning?

One very useful tool for implementing a balanced language program is thematic planning. By choosing a theme with correlating literature selections for a unit of study, a teacher can plan activities throughout the day that lead to a cohesive, in-depth study of the topic. Students will be practicing and applying their skills in meaningful contexts. Consequently, they will tend to learn and retain more. Both teachers and students will be freed from a day that is broken into unrelated segments of isolated drill and practice.

Why Internet Extenders?

Internet extenders have been added to this book to enhance and enrich the learning process. Using key words and phrases, students can access supplemental information to expand their knowledge of the topic while making themselves aware of the many valuable resources to be found on the Internet.

To simplify the process and assure success in locating Web sites, key words and phrases have been provided which can be typed into the search bar of your preferred search engine. You may need to provide some instruction on performing a key word search before assigning Internet Extender activities.

Some Web sites lend themselves to individual or small group research while others are best viewed by the entire class. If one is available, use a large-screen monitor when the entire class is viewing the Web

Internet Extender

Rise and Fall of the Roman Empire (Teacher Information)

Search these key words or phrases: Decline and Fall Roman Empire, Edward Gibbons

The Decline and Fall of the Roman Empire, written in six volumes by Edward Gibbons between 1776 and 1778, describes why the Roman Empire came to an end. On the Internet you will be able to access a synopsis of Gibbon's ideas which can be used as a basis for class discussion. Advanced students may wish to compare the Roman way of life with life in the modern United States.

Roman History

Summary

The history of ancient Rome is presented in a rough chronological order: founding, kingdom, republic, empire, and decline. The traditional story of the founding of Rome by Romulus is followed by a brief activity related to the kingdom. The republican period has many interesting events for modern students who can compare their own democratic institutions with the Roman Republic. Augustus, the empire, and research activities related to the emperors are included.

Here is a suggested plan for the chronological periods in Roman history. You may adapt the ideas to meet needs in your classroom.

Sample Plan

Day 1

- Use Roman vocabulary words (page 14).
- Write about ancient Rome (page 13).
- Label a map of Italy (page 17).
- Research Romulus and Remus (page 18).
- List the Etruscan contributions to Rome (page 19).
- Begin a time line (pages 15–16).

Day 2

- The Roman Republic begins (page 20)
- Complete Pompeii (page 9).
- Find hidden words in the Early Rome Word Search (page 21).
- Distinguish between Athenian democracy and the Roman Republic (page 23).
- Decide whether or not to be king (page 24).
- Solve a crossword puzzle about the Punic Wars (page 25).
- Conduct a trial by jury (page 22).

Day 3

- Distinguish facts from opinions (page 12.)
- Write about your foreign adventure (page 26).
- Decide what to do about Julius Caesar (page 27).
- Identify events associated with Caesar Augustus (page 28).
- Complete When in Rome (Do as the Romans Do) (page 10).

Day 4

- Celebrate a Roman triumph (page 29).
- Learn about the decline and fall (page 30).
- Review famous people in Roman history (page 31).
- Complete the time line (page 16).
- Start a creative writing project (page 13).
- Create a birthday time line (page 33).
- Explore the rise of Christianity in the Roman world (page 32).
- Play the Who Will Be Emperor? Game (pages 73-76).
- Complete Religion in Rome (page 11).

Overview of Activities

Source Books for Roman History

The first half of this unit focuses on the events and people who shaped history. Because there are many texts and other sources available which cover the major events of Roman history, no single source is specified. The list below provides a number of excellent sources for use in your classroom. Make a variety of materials available, and students will be able to compare treatments of individual topics and explore specific areas in depth.

> James, Simon. *Ancient Rome*. Alfred A. Knopf, 1990.
> This book consists of captioned photographs of real and reconstructed artifacts from Roman history. This hardback book should be purchased to use with this unit of study.

> McKeever, Susan. *Ancient Rome*. Dorling Kindersley, 1995.
> This Pockets Full of Knowledge Book contains fascinating facts and art that fit handily into a pocket or backpack.

These books may take some time to locate at a library but will serve as excellent resources for this unit.

> Casilli, Giovanni. *In Search of Pompeii*. Peter Bedwick Books, 1999.
> Contains chronology and Who's Who in Pompeii lists, focuses on the discovery of the buried city. 44 pp.

> Corbishley, Mike. *Everyday Life in Roman Times*. Franklin Watts, 1994.
> Contains detailed information about daily life, nicely illustrated. 32 pp.

> Rice, Melanie and Christopher. *Pompeii, The Day a City was Buried*. D K Publishing, 1998.
> Facts, illustrations and photos of Pompeii artifacts, includes scientific information about volcanoes. 48 pp.

> Roberts, Paul. *Ancient Rome*. Time-Life Books, 1997.
> Examines life in the expanding Roman Empire. 63 pp.

> Sheehan, Sean and Pat Levy. *The Ancient World*, Rome. Raintree, 1999.
> Contains Roman timeline and glossary of terms and lots of information about life in early Rome. 63 pp.

> Steele, Philip. *The Romans and Pompeii*. Dillon Press, 1994.
> Good photos and easy-to-read text. 32 pp.

> Tanka, Shelley. *The Buried City of Pompeii*. Hyperion, Madison Press, 1997.
> A first person account of what it was like when Vesuvius exploded. 48 pp.

Setting the Stage

1. Compare Roman and U.S. coins to spark student interest. Write the words "E pluribus unum," the motto of the United States, on the board. Ask students what language the motto is written in and ask them to look up its meaning.

2. Introduce the topic of ancient Rome by showing the classic movie *Ben Hur*, or at least the chariot race segment, which takes 20 minutes. *Spartacus,* or another film from the list on page 64, may help create student interest.

Overview of Activities *(cont.)*

Setting the Stage *(cont.)*

3. Brainstorm with the whole class. Discuss what they know about Rome. Have each student list everything he or she knows about life in ancient Rome. Staple each list to the inside of a file folder, write the student's name on the tab, and save for future use. The file folders can be used to store samples of student work.

4. Provide some background information about Rome. Make a large mural-sized map of the Roman Empire. If students cannot draw the map, make a transparency of the map on page 59.

5. Recite the Pledge of Allegiance. Ask students what the word *republic* means. Introduce the idea that Rome had a government that was similar to that of the United States in many ways. Discuss the idea of representative government and contrast it with the idea of pure democracy.

Enjoying Roman History

1. Play vocabulary games with the word list on page 14. Look up definitions or give oral clues. Scramble the letters of a famous Roman name and have students unscramble them.

2. Play Caesar by substituting the correct word from the list for the word *Caesar* in the sentences on page 30.

3. Make a large time line that can be expanded as you progress through the unit. Use reference books and the time line checklist on page 15 to start this continuing project.

4. Make Roman tunics. Use pillowcases or sheets to create Roman clothing by following the pattern on page 67. These can be worn by students who attend a dinner party, recite Latin songs, or dramatize events in Roman history.

5. From the list on page 13, choose writing projects that are suitable for the students in your class. Allow the students to read aloud or act out their writing projects while wearing tunics.

6. Complete Pompeii page 9. Assign topics for students projects to be presented to the class.

7. Complete When in Rome (Do as the Romans Do) page 10 as a homework assignment.

Internet Extender

Antique Roman Recipes

Search these key words or phrases: antique Roman dishes, ancient Roman recipes, Roman feasts

Use the Internet to find a number of interesting recipes from Ancient Rome, complete with translations for new terms and measurement conversions to modern methods. Dishes include hamburgers, dessert, fish, fruit, seafood, and pancakes. Have students follow some of these recipes to prepare a Roman feast.

Overview of Activities *(cont.)*

Extending the Unit

1. Create mathematics problems which require students to change from *denarii* to *sestertii*. See page 66 for examples. Make cardboard or tagboard coins and have students exchange denarii for sestertii.

2. Stage a Roman triumph following the events on page 29. Have students parade through the room as victorious soldiers. Other students can cheer. Captives will be "strangled" after the parade.

3. Let students act out the story of Cincinnatus on page 24. Designate some students to be citizens calling Cincinnatus to lead them and others to be citizens who try to convince him to stay on as king after the enemies of Rome are defeated. A third group of students can act as the threatening enemy soldiers who are defeated by Cincinnatus' army.

4. Draw an arch, following the suggestions on page 56. Make a triumphal arch from a refrigerator box or simply draw a building with arches (collosseum, aqueduct, or house). Use a compass to make a nice, smooth, curved line and graph paper to help make the adjoining straight lines.

5. Make a crossword puzzle with ten Roman words. Let students use a computer program or ruler and pencil to create a crossword puzzle. Make up clues. An example of a Hannibal puzzle is on page 25. Students can exchange puzzles, try to solve their neighbor's puzzle, and then return the completed puzzle to its author so that it may be graded.

6. List equal "laws" for all. Have students post school rules or classroom rules on 12 tables (charts) in the classroom. Include the consequences for following/not following the rules on your charts. Let students put rules in their own words, such as "Do your homework."

7. Dramatize a trial by jury. Have students conduct a mock trial for an infraction of school or classroom rules. Appoint a defendant, judge, attorneys, and jurors, following suggestions on page 22.

8. Distribute Religion in Rome page 11 to be read as a group. Assign projects to be completed independently, with a partner, or by small groups.

9. Play the Who Will Be Emperor? Game on pages 73–76. Roll the dice and draw omen cards to see who gets to be emperor of Rome. Keep taking turns until one player goes around the track two times and wins the right to wear the imperial purple.

Internet Extender

Map of the Roman Empire

Search these key words or phrases: map of Ancient Rome, map of Roman Empire, illustrated history of the Roman Empire

Print a map of the Empire from the Internet or examine various cities, territories, and changes to the Empire that occurred over time using interactive maps.

Pompeii

The city of Pompeii was destroyed when a powerful volcano, Mt. Vesuvius, erupted on August 24, A.D. 79. A dark cloud of smoke and ash quickly covered the city and caught its people by surprise. Many escaped, but thousands of other were burned by the fires or crushed by falling debris. In 1592, workers digging a tunnel discovered some of the basements, buildings, and statues of Pompeii, but they were not interested. In 1689, a stone with the inscription *Pompeia* was discovered in the ruins. Many years later, in 1864, an archeologist named Guiseppe Fiorelli began excavating the site and recording its treasures. Since that time there has been an ongoing effort to unlock the secrets of Pompeii.

It was Fiorelli who devised a method for reconstructing the people and animals lost at Pompeii. He found their bodies had decomposed under layers of ash that later hardened into lava rock. Fiorelli carefully filled the open spaces with liquid plaster and was able to recreate exact castings that showed the people in great detail.

Archeologists know that Pompeii was a walled city of about 145 acres. Excavations have revealed temples, markets, shops, a sports center, a theater, public baths, and the best preserved forum of any ancient Roman city.

Today historians know a lot about the structure of Pompeian society. Everyone learned to read and write. There were organized sports and a strong interest in the arts. Many wealthy people had slaves to take care of their property. Their homes were carefully decorated and examples of comfortable furniture and fine clothes had been discovered.

Research Topics: Choose one of the topics to study further. To find information on the Internet, search any of the key words or phrases show in the bold type. Write a one page report on your topic or create an art project for display showing what you have learned.

1. What is a **volcano**? Explain why a volcano erupts and makes a map showing some of the world's most active volcanoes.

2. What is known about **Herculaneum**, a neighboring city which was also destroyed by the A.D.79 eruption of **Mt. Vesuvius**?

3. Who were **Pliny the Younger** and **Pliny the Elder**? What were their contributions to the history of Pompeii?

4. Draw a diagram and explain the function of each room in a typical **Roman public bathhouse**.

5. What excavation is currently being done at Pompeii? How has **technology** changed the work of **archeologists**?

6. **Pompeii** was a busy city. Explain five activities that might have taken place at the **forum**, the center of government.

When in Rome
(Do as the Romans Do)

Most of us live in private homes or apartments. We have comfortable furniture, stylish clothing and adequate food. Each morning we go to public or private schools and our adult family members go to work. We obey the law and respect our elected government officials. Many of us regularly attend a house of worship. In our leisure time, we may participate in various forms of entertainment.

The same statements are true of the ancient Romans. Use reference books or the internet to find Roman contributions that have influenced our daily life.

1. Latin language _____

_____

_____

2. Entertainment _____

_____

_____

3. Government/Politics _____

_____

_____

4. Architecture _____

_____

_____

5. Religion _____

_____

_____

6. Food _____

_____

_____

7. Housing _____

_____

_____

8. Clothing _____

_____

_____

9. Education _____

_____

_____

10. Arts and Crafts _____

_____

_____

On the back of this paper, write a paragraph explaining a typical day in the life of a child in ancient Rome. Draw two pictures to illustrate your story.

Religion in Rome

Ancient Romans were *polytheistic*, meaning they believed in many gods or deities. This group of twelve gods: Jupiter, Juno, Minerva, Vesta, Ceres, Diana, Venus, Mars, Mercury, Neptune, Volcan, and Apollo were especially honored by the Romans. Worshipers offered prayers, food, wine, and animal sacrifices to these and many lesser gods whom they believed controlled everything they did in daily life. Priests and priestesses guarded the temples and conducted religious ceremonies.

Another part of traditional Roman religion involved the daily worship of a different group of household gods. Most private homes had small altars where the head of the family performed daily religious rituals which included honoring dead relatives. Romans also believed that natural events, like a volcano eruption or thunderstorm were messages from the gods and that trees, rocks, and streams had spirits.

Ancient Romans believed that after death they went to the underworld, called Hades. Depending on the time, people chose to be either buried or cremated. As the Empire expanded, Romans were introduced to Judaism and Christianity. These religions permitted the worship of only one god which posed a threat to the Roman government. Judaism and Christianity were banned until A.D. 391 when Christianity was declared the state religion.

Use reference books or these key words or phrases to search the Internet for more information: Roman Gods and Goddesses, ancient Roman religion, Jupiter, Juno, Minerva, Vesta, Ceres, Diana, Venus, Mars, Mercury, Neptune, Vulcan, Apollo, Judaism, Christianity in ancient Rome

Choose one assignment to complete alone, with a partner or group:

- Write a brief report explaining the history of one or more of the Roman gods or goddesses.

- Write an original story including information about the influence of at least one of the deities.

- Design a household altar. Explain how it is used and its significance to the family.

- Create a wall chart with factual information about the twelve most important gods.

- Research information to explain the changes that occurred in Rome when Christianity was declared the state religion. Present your findings in the form of a newspaper or news broadcast.

- Make a poster-sized drawing of an ancient Roman funeral procession.

Fact or Opinion?

Facts are statements about real things or events on which people can agree. For example, "Julius Caesar was assassinated in Rome" is a fact and can be verified. Opinions are statements expressing beliefs or feelings that cannot be proven. For example, "Julius Caesar was the noblest Roman of them all" is an opinion. People can disagree with such a statement. Opinions often use words like "could," "should," "best," and "worst" to express judgements about things.

See whether you can find the facts and opinions in the statements below. Write **F** beside facts and **O** beside opinions. Note: There are no "false facts," just facts and opinions in the list below.

1. _____ The Roman Empire extended around the Mediterranean Sea.

2. _____ Hannibal could have defeated Rome if he had only left his elephants home.

3. _____ The Tiber River runs through Rome.

4. _____ Rome began as a kingdom and then became a republic.

5. _____ Roman soldiers built roads across the empire.

6. _____ Aqueducts never carried the best clean water.

7. _____ Nero was the worst emperor Rome ever had.

8. _____ Augustus Caesar was the best emperor Rome ever had.

9. _____ Rome fell apart after Germanic tribes invaded the empire.

10. _____ The emperor Constantine made Christianity the official religion of the Roman Empire.

11. _____ Public baths were popular in Rome.

12. _____ Roman gods and goddesses were superior to Greek gods and goddesses.

13. _____ Consuls, tribunes, and senators all were government officials during the Roman Republic.

14. _____ The eastern empire, based in Constantinople, was better than the western empire, based in Rome.

Extension: On the back of this paper, write five complete sentences that are facts about Rome and five that are opinions. Have your class determine whether they are facts or opinions.

Creative Writing Activities

Here are some ideas for writing with a Roman theme. Brainstorm with students before giving them an assignment so they can begin to get some ideas together.

Compile student work into individual or class books and display them in the school or classroom library. Include artwork.

1. Tell the story of the life of Julius Caesar. Include his military accomplishments, his reforms, his enemies, and his assassination.

2. Write a confidential and personal letter to Julius Caesar, warning of the plot to assassinate him. Tell him who the conspirators are, the date, and places to avoid. Explain how important his leadership is and how you do not want to see him die.

3. Describe the triumphal march of a victorious Roman general into the city. Include descriptions of the soldiers, the captives, the crowds, and the general himself.

4. Look at the vocabulary list and try to find rhyming words for five words on the list. Then write a rhyming poem about Rome.

5. Pretend you are living in ancient Rome. As you progress through the unit, make journal entries about events. You may choose to be a patrician, plebian, slave, senator, or soldier. Be sure to begin by telling who you are and what daily life is like for you.

Internet Extender

Challenge students to create a play or art project that explains what happened to Pompeii after visiting related sites on the Internet. Have them print maps and pictures from the Web to use in their projects.

Mt. Vesuvius and Pompeii

Search these key words or phrases: Pompeii, Mt. Vesuvius, Herculaneum, Pompeii Forum Project, Pictures of History – Pompeii, Roman Architecture

You will find the Internet has extensive information to use in your projects. It is possible to view photographs of the towns of Pompeii and Herculaneum as well as the volcano that destroyed them in A.D. 79.

Vocabulary

Use this list as a word bank for creative writing, including rhymes and poems; as a vocabulary study for social studies; and as a model for spelling. Add more words to the list as you study ancient Rome.

Places

Rome	Italy
Pompeii	Israel
Carthage	Egypt
Troy	Mediterranean Sea
Gaul	Tiber River

Gods and Goddesses

Jupiter	Mercury
Mars	Saturn
Juno	Venus
Janus	Minerva
Neptune	Vesta

Famous People

Romulus	Horatio
Augustus	Cincinnatus
Julius Caesar	Caligula
Nero	Cicero
Remus	Alaric
Constantine	Pompey
Hannibal	Mark Antony
Jesus	Tarquin

Government Terms

consul	triumph
senate	king
patrician	republic
plebian	censor
tribune	emperor
veto	citizen
Twelve Tables	legionary
dictator	Pax Romana

Other Terms

forum	A.D.	Via Appia	dome
empire	B.C.	concrete	arch
arch	baths	Sabine	gladiator
Etruscans	atrium	toga	sestertius
assassination	chariot	aqueduct	denarius
barbarian	Circus Maximus	pantheon	decline and fall
Latin	colosseum	Vatican	

Checklist for Time Line

How many of these dates can you find in your reading? When you find the date of an event, write it on the corresponding line. Transfer the dates to your time line. Add pictures of facts from your reading to make your time line interesting.

1. Octavian (Augustus) claims title of *princeps* and becomes the first emperor _____
2. Last king of Rome expelled, republic established_____
3. Rome falls in the west_____
4. Pompeii destroyed by a volcano in _____
5. Edict of Milan—freedom of religion_____
6. Rome founded _____
7. Crucifixion of Jesus_____
8. Rule of Nero _____
9. First Punic War _____
10. Second Punic War (Hannibal attacks) _____

Find the year these sites became provinces of the Roman Empire:

11. Achaea (*Southern Greece*) _____
12. Germania Superior_____
13. Judaea (*Israel*) _____
14. Africa (*Carthage and surroundings*) _____
15. Asia (*Western Turkey*) _____
16. Aegyptus (*Egypt*)_____
17. Britannia (*England*)_____

Find approximate years of birth (b.) and death (d.) for the following people:

18. Julius Caesar   b. _____   d._____
19. Augustus Caesar   b. _____   d._____
20. Tarquin   b. _____   d._____
21. Cicero   b. _____   d._____
22. Romulus   b. _____   d._____
23. Constantine   b. _____   d._____

These events and people are suggestions. Add the dates of any events and important people you find in your reading.

Creating a Time Line of Roman History

Because this section of the unit utilizes a variety of sources, a time line will help students organize the information in a chronological sequence.

Materials: Copies of the checklist on page 15, continuous paper, meter or yard stick, markers, reference material

Directions:

1. Divide the class into groups of four or five. Explain that each group will have the opportunity to record the events of Roman history on a time line. If students are unfamiliar with time lines, explain the concept.

2. Discuss the five major periods of Roman history: *founding, kingdom, republic, empire,* and *decline.* Explain that the time lines will show details of each period and the order of events.

3. Decide how much room there is for each time line. Have students measure the space. Point out that the story of Rome begins in 753 B.C. and ends in A.D. 476, a span of 1,200 years. Label the left end of each line 800 B.C. and the right end A.D. 500 Measure and divide the space between these points by 12 and label them as centuries. Explain to students that time is measured in relation to the birth of Christ, which is considered as 0. Events prior to that are labeled B.C. (before Christ) and those after are A.D. (*anno domini* or "year of our lord"). Divide each century into 10 equal spaces to represent decades.

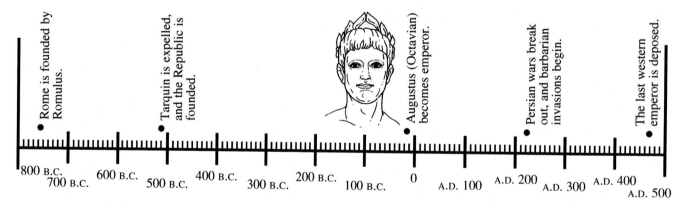

4. Begin by placing the following events on the time line:

   753 B. C.   Rome is founded by Romulus (traditional date).

   509 B. C.   Tarquin is expelled, and the Republic is founded.

   27 B. C.   Augustus (Octavian) becomes emperor.

   A. D. 230   Persian wars break out, and barbarian invasions begin.

   A. D. 476   The last western emperor is deposed.

5. Encourage students to add illustrations or explanations of their time line entries to make them more meaningful.

Where Did the Roman Empire Start?

Can you explain how a city (Rome) conquered the land all around the Mediterranean Sea? It all started with a tribe of Latins who lived in Latium. On the Tiber River, some members of the tribe founded a city which they named Rome after Romulus, the founder. Using an atlas or other maps, label these early sites in ancient Rome's history:

Genoa	**Latium**	**Corsica**	**Sicily**
Florence	**Rome**	**Sardinia**	**Africa**
Etruria	**Tiber River**	**Carthage**	**Mediterranean Sea**

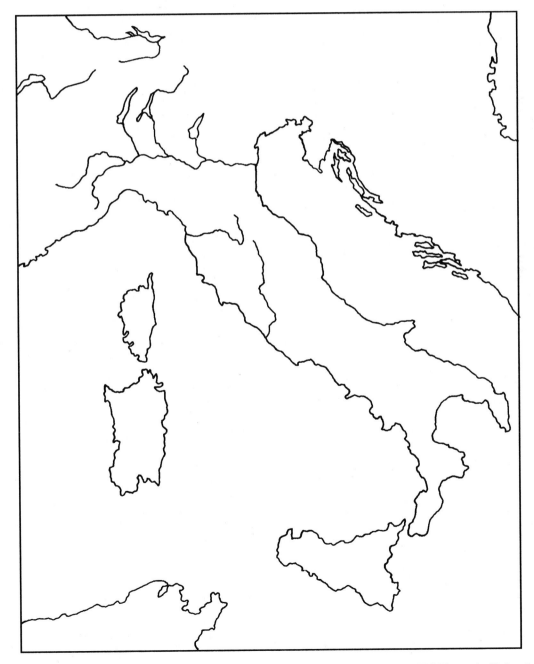

Romulus and Remus

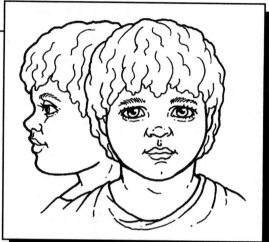

The history of Rome begins with the legend of Aeneas, a Trojan warrior who survived the fall of his city to the Greeks. He wandered for seven years before he settled with the Latins, a tribe on the Italian peninsula. Aeneas married Lavinia, daughter of the Latin king, became king himself, and had a son, Aeneas Silva, who founded the city of Alba Longa, 19 miles from the site of Rome.

Alba Longa became the capital of Latium and was ruled by Aeneas' descendants. One of the kings felt threatened by his brother's twin grandsons, Romulus and Remus, who were said to be sons of the god Mars. The king ordered the infant twins drowned in the Tiber River. Miraculously, they washed ashore where they were suckled by a she-wolf and later raised by a shepherd, Faustulus.

When they were grown, Romulus and Remus returned to Alba Longa, took revenge on the evil king who tried to drown them, and then set out to build their own city. They argued about where to settle; Romulus won the argument by killing his brother, after which he gave his own name to the new city, Rome.

1. What city was the capital of Latium before Rome was built? _____

2. Which of the twin brothers won the argument about where to settle? _____

3. Who was the legendary ancestor of Romulus and Remus? _____

4. What miracle occurred, according to the legend? _____

    _____

    _____

5. Into what tribe did Aeneas marry after the fall of Troy? _____

6. About 1184 B.C., Troy fell. In 753 B.C., Rome was founded. How many years passed from the fall of Troy to the founding of Rome? _____

Critical Thinking: Who founded your city? The United States? Was there fighting over who would be the leader? Write your answers on the back of this paper.

Etruscans—
They Gave Rome Many Things

The later-day Romans were proud of the fact that they threw out the one-man rule of the kings. They replaced it with a *republic,* a representative government, which established a number of officials to lead the country. Consuls, tribunes, and, in times of military emergency, dictators. Rich patricians and more modest plebeians were able to participate in the government.

Many of the things we associate with the republic began under the six kings. A *senatus*, or senate, was a council of elders to advise the king. The popular assembly, the Comitia Curiati, was made up of all citizens capable of bearing arms.

The last three of the kings were Etruscans from the area in northern Italy we now call Tuscany. Many things we associate with Roman culture actually came from the Etruscans: they adopted Greek gods and the legends that went with them, adapted the Greek alphabet, and designed the forum. The forum was a town square drained with Etruscan engineering skills through a *Cloaca Maxima*—Great Sewer. Etruscans built the first *Circus Maximus*—a race track. They also passed on words, music, and clothing (togas, for example) to the Romans.

Activity: Write a persuasive composition to convince a Roman in the republican period that he owes most of his way of life to the "tyrant" Tarquin the Proud and the other Etruscan kings who preceded him. The composition is started for you below:

Dear Friends and Romans,

Even though we know that Tarquin was a bad king, the Etruscans gave us a lot of good things. For example, under their kings we had a senatus, a group of men to advise the king. Also,

_____

_____

_____

_____

_____

_____

_____

_____

_____

_____

Down with Tarquin!

In 509 B.C. the citizens of Rome overthrew their king, Tarquin. He was the last king. The Romans did not want one-man rule. They wanted power in the hands of a group of representatives, a republic.

Activity: Create a dialogue between two Romans who are conspiring to overthrow Tarquin. Let one, Publius, be doubtful. Let the other, Sergius, be ready to fight. Sergius is convinced that one-man rule is bad and if a king has all the power, it will corrupt him. "Power corrupts, absolute power corrupts absolutely." Let Sergius convince Publius that a republic, where representatives of the people have a say, is a better way to run the government. The dialogue is already begun. Add your ideas to finish it.

Sergius: Come on, Publius, you know Tarquin does not deserve to be king! Join us, and we'll get rid of him.

Publius: What? You think he will go without a fight? What has he done that is so bad that I should risk my life to get rid of him?

Sergius: For one thing, he does not listen to the senatus. He just does whatever he wants to do without asking anybody.

Publius: _____

_____

Sergius: _____

_____

Publius: _____

_____

Serguis: _____

_____

Publius: _____

_____

Early Rome Word Search

Circle the key words from the early days of Rome. You will find the answers written left to right and top to bottom. Clues are found below.

L	C	A	X	O	N	S	R	V	E	T	O	P	Z
B	O	B	Y	G	R	E	E	K	S	A	A	N	N
N	N	O	N	D	O	T	P	H	E	W	O	R	P
O	S	Q	Z	Y	M	W	U	D	B	E	C	A	L
S	U	P	M	P	U	D	B	S	E	N	A	T	E
U	L	K	E	L	L	D	L	F	L	E	S	R	B
H	S	I	A	Z	U	N	I	E	L	T	A	I	I
A	E	N	E	A	S	P	C	M	O	N	G	B	A
C	E	G	K	L	A	T	I	N	S	O	O	U	N
A	L	S	R	P	A	T	R	I	C	I	A	N	S
E	I	S	E	S	O	N	Y	N	N	U	R	E	U
P	D	D	P	M	S	I	R	U	Q	E	O	S	S

Clues:

1. King of the Latins before Rome was founded
2. Founder of Rome
3. Rome got her alphabet from the . . .
4. Common people
5. Represent plebeians
6. Rome's rulers before the republic
7. Rule by the people
8. "I forbid"
9. Two powerful officials
10. Tribe that founded Rome
11. Rome's rich upper class
12. King's council of elders
13. Hannibal's mountain challenge

Sentences/Stories:

☆ On the back of this paper write three questions and three statements about early Rome.

☆ Write a story about the founding of Rome or the early Roman government.

Trial by Jury

The *patricians* were the wealthy Romans who ran the Senate and held most of the positions of power. *Plebeians* demanded reforms so that they could not be treated unfairly in law courts or in the making of new laws. The position of *tribune* was created so the plebeians would have a spokesman with the power to *veto,* or reject, laws that were deemed unfair to plebeians.

Another reform was the writing and posting of the Twelve Tables, basic laws for Roman citizens that applied to everyone, patrician and plebian alike. According to the law, Romans were innocent until proven guilty. In criminal cases, a jury trial was held.

Have students conduct a trial of a student accused of some school infraction (running in the hall, for example). Choose a judge, witnesses, and attorneys. Explain that in Roman times the number of jurors depended upon the seriousness of the crime and that early jurors often were victims of or witnesses to the crime. The remaining members of the class will serve as the jury. The mock trial should include a call to order, attorneys questioning witnesses, and a vote by the jury on guilt or innocence.

Sequence of Events in a Trial

1. Call to order (judge)
2. Opening statements
   a. Prosecuting attorney: Jurors, I will prove the defendant guilty of _____ by showing (witnesses, evidence).
   b. Defense attorney: I will prove my client innocent by showing he/she did not do it because (witnesses, evidence).
3. Prosecution witnesses

   a. Witness 1

   questioning by prosecuting attorney

   cross-examination by defense attorney

   b. Witness 2

   questioning by prosecuting attorney

   cross-examination by defense attorney
4. Defense witnesses

   a. Witness 1

   questioning by defense attorney

   cross-examination by prosecuting attorney

   b. Witness 2

   questioning by defense attorney

   cross-examination by prosecuting attorney
5. Closing statements
   a. Prosecuting attorney
   b. Defense attorney
6. Jury deliberation
7. Jury foreman announces verdict

Democracy or Republic?

Athens, Greece, has been called the cradle of democracy. There, for a time, all free, property-owning men could vote in a public assembly to make laws for the city-state. Rome, by contrast, never was governed by such a direct democracy. The Roman republic was governed by a senate, consuls, tribunes, and other elected officials. The representatives made the laws, not the general public.

Read an encyclopedia article about early Rome to understand how their republican government worked. It may help to check on the meanings of the following terms:

consuls _____

plebeians _____

republic _____

veto _____

Tarquin _____

Etruscans _____

patricians _____

kings _____

Twelve Tables _____

dictator _____

tribunes _____

1. Rome expanded around the Mediterranean Sea. Athens did not. From these two examples, does a republic or a democracy seem to be more workable for a growing and expanding empire? Why?

    _____

2. Do you think the United States government is more like Athens or more like Rome? Why?

    _____

3. Did Athenian democracy or the Roman republic grant equality to all people?

    _____

4. Does the United States grant equality for all people? Do we really live up to the words of the "Pledge of Allegiance" that announce a republic with "liberty and justice for all"?

    _____

Critical Thinking: Is it easier to make a quick decision under a king, in a democracy, or in a republic? Why? Is a republic a simpler or more complicated form of government than a kingdom? Is it simpler than direct democracy? Answer these questions on the back of this paper.

Cincinnatus, the Man Who Would Not Be King

After driving out the last king in 509 B.C., Romans began a republic, a government run by elected representatives of the people. The republic was far from perfect, but it worked for about 500 years.

The problem with representative governments is that sometimes a dictator is needed to make quick decisions necessary to defend the people in time of war. In emergencies, Romans appointed a dictator.

One of the most famous dictators was Lucius Quinctius Cincinnatus. He had a small farm on the bank of the River Tiber where he spent most of his time. Once in 458 B.C. and again 439 B.C., Cincinnatus was asked to take over Rome to defend it from enemy attack. He served as dictator, defeating the attackers both times, and many people wanted to make him king. Cincinnatus refused, preferring his quiet home on the farm to high honors and wealth. Cincinnatus was loyal to the republic. You may read more about this real hero who refused to be king in an encyclopedia or in *The Book of Virtues,* by William Bennett, pages 671–674.

What would you do if you became a hero and you were offered a chance to become king? Would you refuse? Why or why not?

_____

_____

_____

_____

_____

George Washington preferred his farm at Mt. Vernon to being president. Some even wanted to make Washington the king of the United States! Why do you think Washington refused to become king after leading the soldiers to victory in the American Revolution? _____

_____

_____

_____

_____

Elephants Go to War!

Rome and Carthage were rival powers in the Mediterranean Sea. Both were expanding trade and military powers in the area. When they came into contact with each other, they fought the Punic Wars. In the first, Rome won Sicily, an island off southern Italy. In the second, the Romans were surprised by an attack from the north. Hannibal, a Carthaginian general, brought elephants with him from Africa and walked them over the mountains of northern Italy. Only after many years of fighting did the Roman army, led by Scipio Africanus, defeat Hannibal and expand the empire.

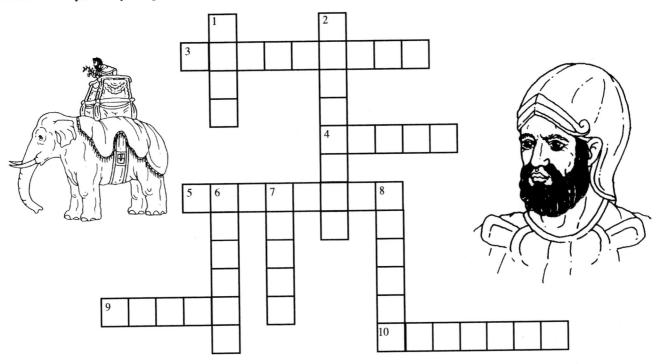

Across

   3. Large African animals
   4. Country Carthage invaded
   5. North African city-state at war with Rome
   9. Elephants were used in the 2nd ___ War.
  10. Rome and Carthage were bitter _____.

Down

   1. Mountains in northern Italy
   2. Carthage's general
   6. Carthage, located in North _____.
   7. Buying and selling
   8. After victory, Rome's _____ expanded.

Activity

On the back of this paper, design a recruiting poster for either Hannibal's elephant-reinforced army or Rome's "defend-our-homeland" army. What would you say to a young man in Carthage to persuade him that he should ride off on an elephant to faraway Italy? What would you say to a Roman who was under attack by these huge beasts? Could you persuade him to stand and fight with the army instead of giving up?

Internet Extender

Roman Battles

Search these key words or phrases: Roman Emperors, Imperial Battles, Ancient Roman Military History, Battles of the Roman Republic

You will understand Ancient Roman military history by accessing these sites.

Foreign Adventure:
I Came, I Saw, I Conquered

One of the most famous phrases in the Latin language is *Veni, vidi, vici* (I came, I saw, I conquered). It was written by Roman military leader and dictator Julius Caesar in his book, *Commentaries on the Gallic Wars*. Caesar conquered Gaul (France) and told the Roman world about his exploits. He described the people of France, the land, and how he conquered the different tribes. Caesar was eager to show everyone what a brave and successful leader of Rome he was.

Imagine that you are visiting a faraway place. You could be a soldier or a tourist. The place you visit could be a real country, or it could be imaginary. Describe what you see to the people back home. Tell what the people are like, what they do, and describe their clothes, customs, and houses.

What is the weather like? What did you do in this foreign land? Tell the story of an adventure. Make sure you are the hero of the adventure and that your story will make you popular with the people who live back in your home town.

My Foreign Adventure

_____

_____

_____

_____

_____

_____

_____

_____

_____

_____

_____

_____

_____

_____

_____

March 15, 44 B.C.
The Assassination of Julius Caesar

You are a Roman senator. Proud of your heritage as a leader of the republic, you are absolutely disgusted with Julius Caesar for having himself appointed dictator for life. It is March 14, 44 B.C. You have been invited to participate in the assassination of the tyrant and restore the true Roman republic. The assassination attempt is scheduled to take place tomorrow, the *ides* (middle day) of March, when Caesar comes to the senate.

Things to consider: Caesar is a hero to many people; he seized power with his army (not exactly legal); he conquered new territory for Rome.

For yourself: You have political enemies who might have you executed for participating in the assassination or defending Caesar. Will you be able to deal with the political situation after the assassination? Will the assassins or the defenders of Caesar be in the majority?

You have one day to decide what you will do. Will you:

1. . . . participate in the assassination attempt? Your ancestors drove out King Tarquin the tyrant. Is "Dictator for Life" any different from "King"?

2. . . . tell Caesar about the plot? You like a stable government without Romans killing other Romans. You want Caesar to be able to defend himself.

3. . . . refuse to participate in the assassination but remain silent about it, hoping it will succeed? You may think that no one, including Caesar, should be made dictator for life, but you worry about the possibility that the assassination attempt will fail and those who participate in it may be executed.

4. . . . take up your sword to defend Caesar because you believe no one should be executed without a fair trial? Even though you think Caesar is wrong to become dictator for life, you believe the Senate and the courts should settle disputes, not assassinations.

On the lines below explain your decision.

_____

_____

_____

_____

_____

_____

Based on your readings in Roman history, tell who would agree with your decision: Mark Antony, Cassius, Brutus, or Octavian (Augustus)? Write your ideas on the back of this paper.

Historically, Cassius and Brutus helped assassinate Julius Caesar. Mark Antony and Octavian were not there to defend him on March 15, but later raised armies to defeat Cassius and Brutus. Still later, Antony and Octavian fought over who would be leader of the empire, with Octavian winning and becoming the first emperor.

Augustus, the First Emperor

Augustus & Julius Caesar

A long series of civil wars followed the assasination of Julius Caesar. Rome was finally united under Julius Caesar's grand nephew and adopted heir, Octavian, who restored peace and stability to Rome. The Senate gave him the name Augustus, which means revered one in Latin. Because Romans hated the title of king, Octavian called himself princeps (the first). Augustus held all the power, although he kept the custom of having consuls elected and continued the Senate. His reign brought peace and property to Rome but cost the people true liberty.

Augustus ruled for 41 years and began the period known as the Pax Romana (Roman Peace), which lasted more than 200 years. He restored law and security, initiated reforms in government, and beautified cities. Many interesting people, places, and things are associated with the reign of the first emperor, Caesar Augustus.

Choose one of these people, places, or things from the Augustan age and research it. Use what you learn to prepare a presentation for the class.

You may choose to recite or act out one of the poems, sculpt a likeness, draw a detailed picture, or build a model.

PEOPLE		**PLACES**	**THINGS**
Cleopatra	Ovid	Altar of Peace	civil service
Virgil	Livy	basilica	Pax Romana
Mark Antony	Maecenas	Pantheon	second triumvirate
Horace	Agrippa	forum	
		Twelve Tables of Law	

Extension: Explain to one of your fellow students why the reign of Augustus is viewed as a Golden Age in Roman history. Tell, in three to five well written sentences, what the first emperor was able to accomplish. Use encyclopedias or other reference books to help you understand his accomplishments.

Art: Pretend that you have just taken a job with the Roman Bureau of Tourism. Your job is to create new "Visit Rome" travel posters. Try sketching the domed Pantheon, the Altar of Peace, or other public buildings. Describe the beautiful marble archways and persuade the tourists to come and see them.

A Roman Triumph

American soldiers, like other soldiers throughout the history of the world, like to parade as heroes for the people back home. After risking their lives in battle, they love to hear the cheers of the hometown crowd. For many soldiers, the public recognition of a special parade makes all the sacrifices seem worthwhile. Roman soldiers liked special parades and ceremonies, too. The honor of a special parade of troops through the city of Rome was reserved for emperors and victorious generals. Fill in the blanks below with the vocabulary of a Roman military triumph. Use the words from the word bank.

When the emperor won a great 1. _____, he would be granted triumph, the right

to lead his 2. _____ through Rome with their 3. _____

and booty. The people lined the streets and 4. _____ for the emperor. A

5. _____ stood behind him, holding a golden 6. _____

over his head. Captured enemy soldiers would be 7. _____ during the

ceremonies. An emperor might want to build a permanent memorial to his glorious victory by

constructing an 8. _____ 9. _____ with his name.

Word Bank		
strangled	archway	prisoners
inscribed	victory	slave
soldiers	crown	cheered

The Decline and Fall

The "Twilight of Rome" (James, pages 62–63) refers to the end of the Pax Romana, or Roman Peace, and the beginning of the Middle Ages. The Empire split into the western and eastern halves. In the west, as a result of economic crisis and military defeats, Roman law and order gave way to a fragmented, more lawless Europe.

Every time you see the word *Caesar* in the sentences below, cross it out and write the correct vocabulary word above it. Choose from the words provided at the bottom of the page.

1. A new *Caesar* religion triumphed in the declining empire.

2. *Caesar* tribes from the north conquered lands formerly held by Rome.

3. Economic chaos and frequent *Caesar* wars between rival generals weakened the empire.

4. The first Christian emperor, *Caesar,* believed that God helped him win his battles.

5. He built a new capital for the empire, *Caesar.*

6. In A.D. 410, Rome itself was *Caesar.*

7. The eastern, or *Caesar,* empire survived many years after the fall of Rome in the west.

8. The city of Rome remained important as a center for the Roman *Caesar* Church.

9. The church continued to use the *Caesar* language.

10. The central figure of the Christian religion, *Caesar,* died on a wooden cross.

11. *Caesar,* the bishop of Rome, negotiated with Attila the Hun and helped save the city from further destruction.

Catholic	the pope	Byzantine
civil	Latin	Christian
Constantinople	Constantine	Jesus Christ
sacked	barbarian	

Heroes of Rome

How well do you know the history of Rome? Do you know the famous people and famous deeds of the ancient Romans?

Review the previous pages of this unit and then try to fill in the blanks below. The first letter of each answer is given. The exact number of blanks is given for spelling out the correct answer.

1. An earlier Brutus than the one who helped assassinate Julius Caesar, expelled the last king of Rome, and set up a new government called a r __ __ __ __ __ __ __

2. Legendary founder of the Roman race, carried his father out of Troy:
   A__ __ __ __ __

3. Adopted son of Julius Caesar and first emperor of Rome: A __ __ __ __ __ __ __

4. Assassin of and former friend of Julius Caesar: B __ __ __ __ __

5. Periods of Roman history: kings, republic, e __ __ __ __ __ __

6. Egyptian queen who challenged Rome: C __ __ __ __ __ __ __ __

7. Founded the greatest city in Europe after killing his brother: R __ __ __ __ __ __ __

8. Dictator and consul of Rome, assassinated on the Ides of March, conquered Gaul:
   J __ __ __ __ __   C __ __ __ __ __

9. Refused to be king or act as dictator for anytime longer than necessary:
   C __ __ __ __ __ __ __ __ __ __ __

10. The last king of Rome, driven out in 509 B.C.: T __ __ __ __ __ __ __

11. Twin brother of Romulus: R __ __ __ __ __

12. Emperor who fiddled while Rome burned: N __ __ __ __

13. Single handedly defended a bridge when Rome was under attack:
    H __ __ __ __ __ __ __

14. Became the first Christian emperor: C __ __ __ __ __ __ __ __ __ __ __

15. Cleopatra's lover: M __ __ __   A __ __ __ __ __ __

16. Founded a new religion; his birthday is the turning point in our calendar:
    J __ __ __ __

17. Used elephants to fight against Rome: H __ __ __ __ __ __ __ __

Christians and the Roman World

When the empire fell apart, the Christian religion remained. The earliest records we have of the relationship between the Roman Empire and Christianity are found in the New Testament section of the Bible. Cities, emperors, governors, and execution methods are documented in the New Testament.

Find an easy-to-read translation of the Bible and look up the answers to the following:

1. Emperor at Jesus' birth (Luke 2:1) _____

   _____

2. The sixth book of the New Testament was sent to the Christians in this city. _____

   _____

3. A Jewish king supported by the Romans (Acts 12:1)

   _____

4. A Roman centurion (military officer) mentioned in (Acts 10:1)

   _____

5. A city used for the Roman government of Palestine (Acts 10:1)

   _____

6. The Roman governor who ordered Jesus' death (Luke 23:1)

   _____

7. A Roman coin used in paying taxes (Matthew 22:19) _____

8. Whose picture is on a Roman coin? (Matthew 22:21) _____

9. Roman method of executing criminals (Luke 23:33)

   _____

10. Why did the Apostle Paul demand certain rights? (Acts 22:25–26)

    _____

Birthday Time Lines

For many years, people around the world have measured time from the birth of Jesus Christ. The year A.D. 1995 means 1,995 years since the birth of Jesus or "the year of our Lord 1995." The year 44 B.C. means 44 years before the birth of Christ. There is no year 0.

When is your birthday? You were probably six years old when you were in first grade. If your name is John, you could say first grade was in the year A.J. 6 (year of John). When did your mom first meet your dad? It might be B.J. 3 (before John was born.)

Make up your own time line of events surrounding your birth. Use "before (your name)" and "after (your name)."

Sample Events for Your Time Line

President Bill Clinton's first election

President George W. Bush's first election

your first tricycle

your first bicycle

your first day in school

your fourth grade teacher's name

Mom and Dad's wedding

Grandma's wedding

brother/sister's birth

when a new building was built

the year a favorite book was published

the year you met your best friend

when you first played a video game

first visit to a place of worship

the year you went on your favorite trip

Ancient Rome
by Simon James

Summary

Romans adopted elements of Greek intellectual and cultural achievements and combined them with their own perspectives. The result was the Greco-Roman tradition which was the core of medieval learning and the inspiration of the Renaissance. When the Roman army conquered other civilizations, it also helped to spread Roman culture throughout the Western hemisphere. Reading Ancient Rome *is like browsing in a museum. It is a picture book of ancient artifacts and drawings of the ancient world which will give students an understanding of daily life in Roman times and the Roman heritage which we all share.*

Sample Plan

Day 1

- Assign creative writing activities (page 13).
- Read pages 6–15. *Emphasis:* soldiers
- Use the Emperors Time Line (page 40).
- Label the legionary chart (page 39).
- Research an emperor (page 41).
- Vote thumbs up/thumbs down for the emperor (page 42).

Day 2

- Continue creative writing activities (page 13).
- Read pages 16–25. *Emphasis:* Roman society
- Match vocabulary about Roman society (page 43).
- Compare women in Rome and America in a composition (page 44).
- Make a tunic (page 67).
- Learn where Latin is used today (page 51).

Day 3

- Continue creative writing activities (page 13).
- Read pages 26–35. *Emphasis:* construction/spectacles
- Name the rooms in a comfortable city house (pages 68–69).
- Find facts about the Colosseum (page 45).
- Put the chariot races in order (page 47).

Day 4

- Continue creative writing activities (page 13).

- Read pages 36–45. *Emphasis:* arts/crafts
- Act out a play/create masks (page 62).
- Take a trip to the baths (page 48).
- Learn to do Roman math (pages 53–55).
- Use Roman crafts to make a mosaic, fresco, or relief (page 61).

Day 5

- Continue creative writing activities (page 13).
- Read pages 46–55. *Emphasis:* daily life
- Have a Roman dinner party (page 37).
- Sing Latin songs (page 63).
- Chart the gods and goddesses (page 49).
- Write and perform a dialogue about Augustus' vow (page 38).

Day 6

- Read pages 56–63. *Emphasis:* decline
- Read Mark Antony's funeral oration (Shakespeare's *Julius Caesar*).
- Solve math problems (pages 65–66).
- Interpret famous sayings (page 50).
- Culminating Activity: Take a Roman holiday (pages 70–72).

Day 7

- Continue creative writing activities (page 13).
- Find the Latin origin of everyday words (page 52).
- Place events in history (page 57).

Chapter Activities

Use the questions and activities on pages 35–38 to help students enjoy *Ancient Rome* by Simon James. Encourage them to use other sources to explore and expand topics introduced in the book.

☞ *City-state to superpower* (page 6)

Discuss: Who were the Etruscans? What did they invent? What Roman customs come from this group? What were Hannibal's most famous battles? How does he compare to Alexander the Great? How did the Romans finally defeat Hannibal?

Activities: Have students do an oral or written report on one of the following: Etruscans, Hannibal, the Punic Wars, or Hannibal and the history of military strategy.

☞ *The emperors* (page 8)

Discuss: Was the change to an emperor necessary? Tell why or why not. What did the Empire accomplish? What made an emperor good or bad?

Activities: Choose an emperor and write a report. Tell about his accomplishments and failures. How did he become emperor? How did he die? (pages 40–42) Sculpt a bust of an emperor from clay or create a portrait of an emperor on paper or in a fresco (page 61), showing what he looked like.

☞ *The legionary; battle and defense* (pages 10–13)

Discuss: Describe the armor and equipment of a Roman soldier. Why was each piece of equipment necessary? What was different about officer uniforms? What were auxiliary regiments, and why were they important?

Activities: Make and label a large poster showing the Roman soldier and his armor (page 39). Research Roman forts and draw a poster or build a model of a fort.

☞ *Soldiers in society* (page 14)

Discuss: How were soldiers paid? What other benefits were there for poorer people and provincials who joined the army? What is a centurion? How did the army keep the peace?

Activity: Make a poster with military vocabulary and matching definitions.

☞ *Senators, citizens, subjects, slaves* (page 16)

Discuss: Did Romans believe that all people were equal? How would you describe Roman clothing and hairstyles? Why was the forum an important place?

Activities: Draw or trace different kinds of clothing worn in Rome. Include people of different social ranks or positions. Make a tunic (page 67). Draw the eagle inscription, "the Senate and the people of Rome," fasces, or a design for a ring. Explain the meaning of your symbol.

☞ *The women of Rome* (page 18)

Discuss: How were Roman women like women today? How were they different?

Activities: Write a descriptive composition telling about the types of jewelry worn in Rome. Compare and contrast the women of ancient Rome with the women of modern America (page 44).

Chapter Activities *(cont.)*

☞ *Growing up; family life; house and home (pages 20–25)* ━━━━

Discuss: What was life like for wealthy children in Rome? What toys did they play with? Did they go to school? Describe the Roman family. What kinds of pets did Romans keep? What was a lar? A genius? Describe a Roman home. What was an atrium? A peristyle? How was it decorated? What was a tenement?

Activities: Describe the way Romans practiced their religion in their homes. Describe what slavery was like in Rome. Name the rooms in a comfortable Roman house (pages 68–69). Make a model of a house or draw a room, showing the decorations and furniture (page 69).

☞ *Builders and engineers (page 26)* ━━━━

Discuss: What lasting construction projects did the Romans produce? What were trademarks of Roman construction? Why does their plumbing seem so modern?

Activities: Construct an arch from clay or blocks, or use heavy poster board to draw an aqueduct or building (basilica, colosseum) and color in the arches.

☞ *A day at the races (page 34)* ━━━━

Discuss: Which was bigger, the Circus Maximus or the Colosseum? What was the procedure for a chariot race?

Activities: Describe a chariot race from start to finish. Write down the steps of the race (see page 47), and then deliver the account to your classroom audience as though you were a sports announcer. Make clay models of chariots and use a mock race track (pages 73–74) to hold a race.

☞ *The theater (page 36)* ━━━━

Discuss: What did Roman actors wear that modern actors do not wear? What kinds of plays did Romans prefer? What types of performances did Romans invent?

Activities: Write a comic scene from a play set in ancient Rome and act it out. Draw the classic comic and tragic masks that have become the symbols for the theater or make a mask from papier mâché (page 62).

☞ *A trip to the baths (page 38)* ━━━━

Discuss: What did the Romans do at the baths besides bathe? Did they use soap? Was the water all the same temperature? What special equipment was used?

Activity: Write a story about a trip to the baths. Give names to the characters and tell what they do there and the equipment that they use. (See page 48.)

Chapter Activities *(cont.)*

☞ *Writing it all down* *(page 40)*

Discuss: How is the Roman alphabet different from our alphabet? How are Roman numbers different from ours? Which system is easier?

Activities: Explore the Latin roots of English words (pages 52). Make a large chart showing Latin words on one side and English words on the other. Let students try to match them up. Make the same kind of matching game out of Roman numbers and our number system. Make up and solve math problems using Roman numbers (page 53).

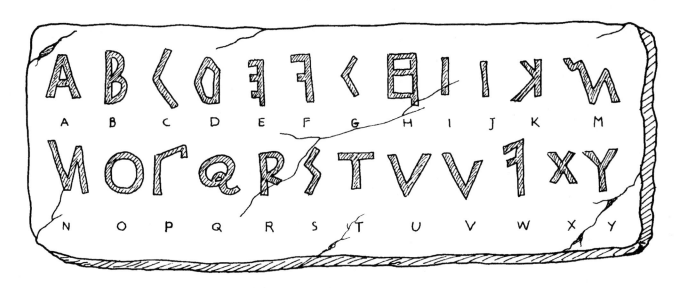

☞ *Craftworkers and technology* *(page 42)*

Discuss: Of what were pots and other table containers made? What kinds of decorative designs were molded or painted on them? How many different kinds of jewelry did Roman women wear?

Activity: Hold a craft fair. Display student-made mosaics, relief sculptures, frescoes (page 61), papier mâché masks (page 62) or other clay objects or jewelry students have made.

☞ *First catch your dormouse* *(page 44)*

Discuss: What did Romans eat? Did rich and poor eat differently? What cooking utensils did the Romans use? Which ones are the same as those we use today?

Activity: Prepare a Roman dinner party or simple "Italian" meal, using popular dishes. Readily available foods include spaghetti, bread, olives, grapes, and cheese.

☞ *Making music* *(page 48)*

Discuss: When did the Romans use music? What kinds of instruments did the Romans use? Do we know what it sounded like?

Activity: Let students demonstrate their musical ability at a poetry reading. Let one student read a poem while others play instruments in the background. This may be combined with the dinner party in the previous chapter.

Chapter Activities *(cont.)*

☞ *A world of many gods; worship and sacrifice (pages 50–53)*

Discuss: Discuss the different religions of the Roman empire. How were some of the gods like the Greek gods? What other "foreign" gods were adopted by Romans? What is a temple? Shrine? Who were the vestal virgins and what did they do? Why were emperors worshipped?

Activity: Write and act out a dialogue between Augustus and one of his friends as the future emperor leaves a temple of Mars and promises to build a new temple to that god if Mars helps him avenge the death of his adoptive father, Julius Caesar.

☞ *Healing the sick (page 54)*

Discussion: What was the connection between healing and religion? What can be healed today that was fatal in Roman times? What herbs were thought to have healing powers?

Activities: Make a chart showing which herbs some people believe have healing potential today or make a chart of foods showing the vitamins that each food contains. Act out a scene in which Aeneas has an arrow removed without anesthetic.

☞ *Death and burial (page 56)*

Discussion: How did Romans bury the dead? Where did they like to bury their ancestors? What happened in Pompeii, Italy, in A.D. 79? Where do we get the idea of "crossing the river" after we die?

Activities: Write and deliver a funeral oration of a famous emperor. Try to think of as many good things he did in his life as can be mentioned. Read aloud Mark Antony's oration in Shakespeare's *Julius Caesar.*

☞ *Country life (page 58)*

Discuss: Why were farms important? What was raised and grown on Roman farms? Why did the rich Romans prefer the countryside? What animals were hunted for food in ancient Rome?

Activities: With information from the wildlife department in your state, make a chart showing hunting seasons for different animals in your area. Plant a tree or start a school garden.

☞ *Transportation, travel, and trade (page 60)*

Discuss: Why is peace necessary for trade? What is prosperity? What were the different ways of traveling and transporting goods? Name the different Roman coins.

Activities: Describe a trip to the forum, the purchases, and the costs of the purchases. Solve some problems that require Roman coin conversions (page 66).

☞ *The twilight of Rome (page 62)*

Internet Extender
Collapse of the Roman Empire
Search these key words or phrases: Collapse of the Roman Empire, History for Kids–The Fall of Rome, Fall of Rome, Decline and Fall of Roman Empire, Ancient Roman Military History
Read about the downfall of the Roman Empire, complete with dates and important people of the

The Legionary

Roman legions were successful in conquering the known world. Soldiers, legionaries, were well equipped with weapons and protective clothing to keep them on the front lines, enforcing the Pax Romana or Roman Peace. Using James, pages 10–11, dictionaries, or other reference books, find pictures of the equipment of the Roman soldier. Draw and label some of the equipment. Use the list at the bottom of the page.

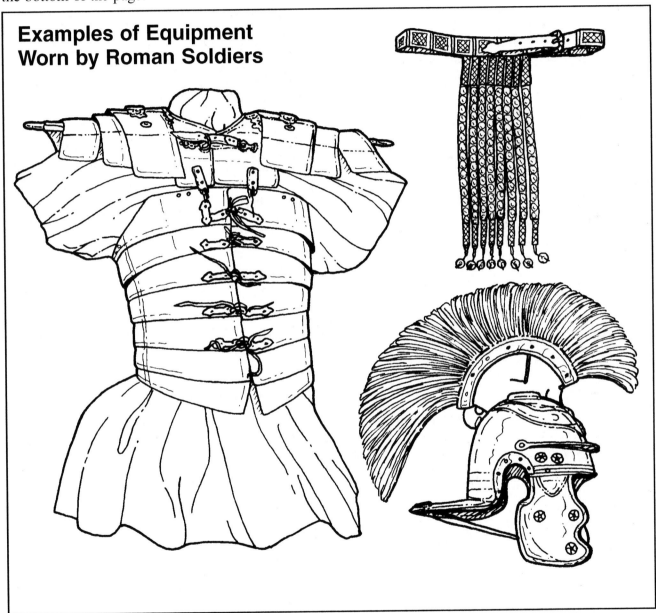

Examples of Equipment Worn by Roman Soldiers

sandals	shield	leg protectors	dagger
crest	breeches	helmet	belt
sword	breastplate	spear	tunic
sheath	harness	shoulder strap	scabbard

Emperors Time Line

Roman emperors are known for their accomplishments or their failures. From first to last, emperors exercised real power in the government of a large land area around the Mediterranean Sea. Use the chart/time line at the right to answer the questions below.

Roman Emperors	
23 B.C. Augustus	**282** Carus
A.D. 14 Tiberus	**283** Carinus and Numerian
37 Gaius (Caligula)	
41 Claudius	*Empire split into four sections under two Augusti and two Caesars*
54 Nero	
68-69 Galba	**284-285** *Diocletian*
69 Otho and Vitellius	**286-305** Maximian
69 Vespasian	**293-296** Constantius Chlorus
79 Titus	
81 Domitian	**293-311** *Galerius*
96 Nerva	**305-307** Flavius Severus
97 Trajan	**308-324** Licinus
117 Hadrian	**306-337** *Constantine I (SoleEmperor of East and West, 324)*
138 Antoninus Pius	
161-180 Marcus Aurelius	**337-340** Constantine II
176-192 Commodus	**337-350** Constans
193 Pertinax	**337-361** *Constantius II*
193-211 Septimius Severus	**361-363** *Julian*
	363-364 *Jovian*
198-217 Caracalla	**364-375** *Valentinian I*
217 Macrinus	**364-378** *Valens*
218 Elagabalus	**367-383** Gratian
222 Severus Alexander	**375-393** Valentinian II
235 Maximin Thrax	**379-395** *Theodosius I*
238 Gordian I, II, III	**385-388** Maximius
244 Philip and others	**392-394** Eugenius
249 Decius and others	**395-423** Honorius
253 Gallienus and others	**425-455** Valentinian III
268 Claudius II	**457-474** *Leo I*
269 Aurelian and others	**475-476** Romulus Augustus
275 Tacitus	*(Eastern Emperors in italics)*
276 Probus	

1. How many emperors are listed on this time line? _____

   Did they all serve an equal number of years?

   _____

2. Who was the first emperor?

   _____

   The last? _____

3. When did the empire split into four sections?

   _____

   When was it reunited under one emperor?

   _____

4. Who served as emperor immediately before Nero? _____

   After Nero? _____

5. Give the years of Marcus Aurelius' reign.

   _____

6. How many emperors were named Constantine?

   _____

   Valentinian? _____

7. How many years passed from the reign of Vespasian to the reign of Gratian? _____

8. Was Tacitus emperor before or after Antoninus Pius? _____

   Before or after Galerius? _____

9. How many years passed from Hadrian's reign to Diocletian's reign? _____

Emperor Report Form

Rome had many emperors over nearly 500 years. Look at the list on page 40 and choose one for a report. Some of the more well-known emperors like Augustus, Claudius, Nero, Trajan, Constantine, Hadrian, Aurelius, Tiberius, Titus, and Caligula will be relatively simple report projects. Others may prove to be more challenging.

What is your emperor's name? _____

What is the name of the emperor he succeeded? _____

What is the name of the emperor who came after him? _____

During which years was your emperor in power? _____

How many years did he serve as emperor? _____

How did he become emperor? _____

What were his accomplishments?

    1. _____

    2. _____

    3. _____

    4. _____

What were his failures?

    1. _____

    2. _____

Was he a good or a bad emperor? (Explain your answer.) _____

_____

_____

How did he die? _____

_____

Internet Extender

Roman Emperors

Search these key words or phrases: Ancient History Roman Biographies, Roman Emperors, Emperors of the Roman Empire, or specific names of individual emperors

Access brief biographical information on many of the Roman Emperors, then choose one emperor to research in depth using the Internet plus other resources and compile the information in a report using the form on this page.

Thumbs Up/Thumbs Down
for the Emperor

Emperors longed to be popular with the people of Rome. One way to accomplish this was to sponsor large gladiator fights and other games in the Colosseum. During the fights, a wounded gladiator could appeal for mercy to the emperor, who, watching the crowd, would give a thumbs up (mercy) or thumbs down (no mercy).

But what if the citizens of Rome were given a vote on the emperor? Would you vote thumbs up for Nero, who "fiddled while Rome burned"? Thumbs down for the mad Caligula?

In the space below, use James, pages 8–9, encyclopedias, or other reference books to name five emperors and then give them a "thumbs up" or "thumbs down" for their performances in office. In the last column, give specific reasons why you liked the emperor (thumbs up) or disliked the emperor (thumbs down).

Pretend that you are emperor. What would you do to be popular with your fellow Romans? Explain what you would do to rate a "thumbs up" as emperor.

Emperor	Thumbs Up? Thumbs Down?	Reason

Senators, Citizens, Subjects, and Slaves

America likes to think of itself as a land of equal opportunity for all. Ancient Rome was not like that—equality was neither an ideal nor a reality. Using pages 16–17 in James or other reference books, match the Roman social classes with some of the telltale signs of their status.

Note: Each set of five words matches with the five phrases directly across from them. Draw lines to correctly match the items. There is no matching beyond the dividing lines.

1. senators	a. senate and people of Rome
2. equestrians	b. highest class of citizens
3. toga	c. senate house
4. curia	d. men's formal wear
5. SPQR	e. less status than senators

6. slaves	a. fashionable, A.D. 130
7. forum	b. brooch, fastens cloaks
8. clipped beard	c. some downtrodden, some not
9. fibula	d. market square
10. gladiator	e. could win freedom in arena

11. rings	a. bundle of rods containing an ax
12. fasces	b. below governor
13. lictors	c. worn by men and women
14. procurator	d. senator, commands army
15. provincial governor	e. official escorts

Women in Rome and America

Women in Rome, if wealthy, had a great deal of status, if not equality with men. Is it true that women have "come a long way"? Use reference books and the chart below to compare the status of women in ancient Rome and modern America (James, pages 19–20, 22). Form your opinion about what life was like for women of the ancient empire as compared to life for women in modern America. Then write a persuasive composition supporting one of the following statements. Begin your composition at the bottom of this page and continue on the back.

❑ American women have a better life than women in ancient Rome.

❑ Roman women had a better life than women in America today.

❑ American women and women in ancient Rome are equals in their quality of life.

Women in Rome	Women in America
expected to run household	expected to run household and/or pursue a job/career
little if any schooling	mandatory education; college available for all
used makeup	use makeup
spun and wove clothing by hand	generally purchase machine-made clothing
wore jewelry	wear jewelry
few professionals—midwives, priestesses, doctors, hairdressers	enter virtually all professions
married in a veil, exchanged vows	marry in a veil, exchange vows
wives of senators and emperors had some political influence	all may vote and may be elected to any political office

_____

_____

_____

_____

_____

_____

The Colosseum

One of the most famous buildings in Rome is the Colosseum. Almost 2,000 years old, its ruins have attracted artists who draw and paint its architectural grandeur. Using *Ancient Rome* by Simon James (pages 28–29) or other reference books, identify the statements below that are true (T) and those that are false (F).

1. _____ The Colosseum opened in A.D. 80.

2. _____ Only animals were killed in the arena.

3. _____ The outside of the Colosseum was decorated with statues.

4. _____ A canvas awning often provided shade.

5. _____ There were only five entrances to the Colosseum.

6. _____ Gladiators fought each other to the death.

7. _____ Only 5,000 people could fit in the Colosseum.

8. _____ The weight of the seating was carried on arches.

9. _____ Emperors paid for bloody fights to gain popularity.

10. _____ The arena could be flooded in order to make a swimming pool.

Imagine that you are a creative and humanitarian Roman emperor and do not like the bloody shows in the Colosseum. Think of an alternative way to entertain the crowds of Rome who love to see a spectacle. You want to provide excitement, enthusiasm, suspense, and surprise. But you definitely want to stop showing the slaughter of human beings as entertainment.

In one well-written paragraph on another page, describe your humane alternative.

Internet Extender

Roman Homes and Buildings

Search these key words or phrases: Ancient Rome: Images and Pictures, Ancient Roman Architecture

Access sites that show the homes and buildings of Ancient Rome.

My New Show for the Old Colosseum

Now that you have a better idea for using the Colosseum without human or animal bloodshed, how will you convince the public that they should come and see your show? Remember, you have to stay popular in order to keep your position as emperor.

On a large poster board, create an advertisement for your new show. Is it a music concert, a drama, or a mock battle using fake weapons? Could it be some sort of athletic contest like football or basketball?

Will it be free to the public (most gladiator contests were)? What will be exciting about the event? How long will the event last? What kind of refreshments will you sell?

Be sure to include the following:

- ❏ **a title** for your event

- ❏ **a time and day** for the event

- ❏ **vivid adjectives** like "exciting," "amazing," "wonderful," to describe the event

- ❏ **a drawing of the Colosseum** itself to let people know where your event will be held

- ❏ **a drawing of the event** itself to arouse interest in attendance

- ❏ **testimonials** from famous or imaginary Roman citizens about how great the event will be and how they plan to attend

- ❏ **convincing statements** about how your event is much superior to bloody gladiator fights

Chariot Races

While the Colosseum held only 50,000 gladiator fans, the Circus Maximus, which served as a chariot racetrack, held up to 250,000 people in an oval shaped stadium. It could be quite an unruly mob, especially since they were divided into four groups of fanatical fans of the Reds, Blues, Greens, and Whites.

Imagine you are telling a friend about the races. He is a little bit confused about the sequence of events during a chariot race. Use James, pages 34–35, or other reference books to explain to him the order of events at the Circus Maximus.

A. The chariots race seven times around, counter-clockwise.

B. They cross the finish line in front of the emperor's box.

C. Spectators place their bets and buy snacks.

D. The winner is given a bag of gold.

E. The horses begin thundering around the spina.

F. Up to 12 chariots line up.

G. The horses paw the ground anxiously.

H. A white cloth is dropped to signal the start.

The correct order is:

1. _____

2. _____

3. _____

4. _____

5. _____

6. _____

7. _____

8. _____

A Trip to the Baths

Look at pages 38–39 in James or another reference book about the Roman baths. Then fill in the blanks to complete the story below.

Lucius and Marcus

Lucius had a long day at the Senate. Before going home, he and his friend Marcus decided to stop at the public (1) _____. They chatted about last week's (2) _____ fight and (3) _____ for a few minutes in the yard. Then they went inside to a (4) _____ , took their clothes off, and went into a (5) _____ pool to sweat. Then they went into a (6) _____ pool to close their pores. Lucius and Marcus were splashed by their slaves who used (7) _____ to rinse off the nobles. They also scraped themselves with (8) _____ and then applied (9) _____ to their bodies when they got out.

Word Bank

paterae	hot water	strigils
baths	cold water	exercised
gladiator	olive oil	changing room

Gods and Goddesses

Today many people are familiar with the gods and goddesses of the Romans, many of whom are almost identical to the gods of the Greeks. Jupiter, the king of the Roman gods, resembled the Greek god Zeus. Using James, pages 50–51, and other reference books, fill in the chart below. Then answer the questions using the back of this paper.

Greek God or Goddess	Roman God or Goddess	Area of Interest
Zeus	Jupiter	Thunder
①	Juno	Wife of Jupiter
②	③	Love, Beauty, Fertility
Athena	④	⑤
Dionysius	⑥	Rebirth, Wine
Poseidon	⑦	The Sea
⑧	Pluto	The Underworld
Apollo	⑨	Light, Truth, Healing
⑩	Mars	War
Artemis	Diana	⑪

1. Why did Romans not tolerate the early Christians?

2. In a dictionary look up the word *polytheism*. Does the word apply to the ancient Roman religion or to the Christian religion which gained many converts in the empire?

3. Look up a definition for the word *monotheism*. What religions are forms of monotheism?

Famous Sayings

The Roman Republic and Roman Empire were around for over 900 years. Famous sayings and proverbs come from this time period.

What do you think each saying or proverb means? Write your ideas on the lines provided.

When in Rome, do as the Romans do. _____

_____

I came, I saw, I conquered. (Julius Caesar) _____

_____

Et tu, Brute—"And you, Brutus." (said by Julius Caesar in Shakespeare's play)

_____

Pax Romana—"Roman Peace" _____

_____

He fiddled while Rome burned. (said of Emperor Nero) _____

_____

Carpe diem—"Seize the day." (written by Horace, poet) _____

_____

Rome wasn't built in a day. _____

_____

All roads lead to Rome. _____

_____

Latin Today

Although many people think that Latin is a "dead" language" because it is no longer spoken, does not create new words, and does not change, the Roman language lives on in several areas. Law and medicine both have their roots in our Roman heritage and use Latin terms. Latin also lives on in science and music.

 Divide the class into six groups. Assign five terms to each group of students. Have them use a dictionary or other reference book to find the meanings of these Latin phrases and report to the class.

Law

1. de facto
2. bona fide
3. de jure
4. habeas corpus
5. status quo
6. prima facie
7. cui bono
8. ex post facto
9. nolo contendere
10. pro bono

Medicine (suffix -ology or -ics means "the study of")

1. anesthesiology
2. cardiology
3. dermatology
4. audiology
5. pediatrics
6. neurology
7. orthopedics
8. radiology
9. urology
10. geriatrics

Music

1. alto
2. piano
3. forte
4. tenor
5. soprano

Other

1. quid pro quo
2. gratis
3. et cetera (etc.)
4. persona non grata
5. per capita

 Critical thinking: Can you explain why these Latin terms continue to be used? What are the advantages of a dead language in these professions? Are there any disadvantages?

How Much Latin Do You Speak?

Some modern languages are called Romance languages because they are based on Latin. Although English is not officially a Romance language, Latin was the language of government, scholarship, and religion in England during the Middle Ages, and many words based on Latin roots and prefixes and/or suffixes became part of English. For a time French, a Romance language, was the court language in England, which added to the Latin influence on English.

Below is a list of word parts with their meanings. By changing the prefix, you can change the meaning of the root. For example: *port* means carry, so *im*–port is to carry in, while *ex*–port is to carry out. What does *trans*–port mean? *Re*–port? *De*–port? Suffixes are sometimes added to the end of a root or word to change its use from a verb to a noun or adjective.

Prefix	**Root**
a, ab, abs *(from, away)*	dic, dict *(say, speak)*
com, con *(together)*	duc, duct *(lead)*
de *(down, away)*	fer *(bear)*
ex, e *(out of)*	ject *(throw)*
in, im *(into, on)*	mit, miss *(send)*
inter, intro *(between)*	port *(carry)*
pre, pro *(before)*	scrib, script *(write)*
re *(back, again)*	spec, spect *(look)*
sub *(under)*	pel *(drive)*
trans *(across)*	gress *(step, go)*

Activity: Use the list above to find the word that means each of the following.

1. down + throw _____

2. under + write _____

3. into + look _____

4. back + send _____

5. before + step _____

6. together + drive _____

7. across + bear _____

8. together + lead _____

9. between + speak _____

Extensions:

Choose one or more roots. Have students brainstorm to see how many words they know that contain the root. List their responses on the chalkboard or make a chart.

Have students write each prefix and root on a card. Use the cards as building blocks to create new words. Challenge a classmate to translate the new words. Check the results in a dictionary to see if there is such a word.

Roman Numerals

The Romans not only gave us many words from Latin that became part of English usage, they also gave us a number system. Here are some examples of Roman numerals.

1 = I	**7 = VII**	**30 = XXX**
2 = II	**8 = VIII**	**50 = L**
3 = III	**9 = IX**	**100 = C**
4 = IV	**10 = X**	**200 = CC**
5 = V	**11 = XI**	**500 = D**
6 = VI	**20 = XX**	**1000 = M**

Notice that to make a number like 324, start with the largest value—hundred or C. Three hundreds = CCC. To add tens, place them to the right of the hundreds. Two tens = XX. 320 = CCCXX. To add ones, if a letter is followed by one of greater value, the first is subtracted from the second. Example: IV = 5 – 1 = 4, add to the right of the tens, 4 = IV, 324 = CCCXXIV.

Try to write these as Roman numbers:

1. 23 _____   3. 78 _____   5. 39 _____

2. 172 _____   4. 876 _____   6. 407 _____

Now try to write the modern numbers for these Roman numerals:

7. XXV _____   9. CCLI_____

8. CXIII _____   10. CCCLXX _____

Solve these mathematics problems, answering in Roman numerals:

11. XX + XVI =_____   14. CVII – X = _____

12. CCL – XXV =_____   15. X x X = _____

13. CXL + XXII =_____   16. XV x IV = _____

On your own: In the space below, write and solve four problems of your own.

A.   B.   C.   D.

Monumental Math

Look at the list of famous monuments to Roman engineering. Then answer the questions on the following page.

Castel Sant' Angelo—built by Emperor Hadrian in A.D. 136 as a tomb for himself and his successors

---

Trajan's Column—97 foot (29.6 m) marble shaft dedicated to Emperor Trajan in A.D. 113

The Pantheon—Rome's only perfectly preserved ancient building; begun by Agrippa in 27 B.C., became a domed, circular temple under Hadrian in A.D. 124, used as a church since A.D. 609

The Colosseum—built about A.D. 80, approximately a third of a mile in circumference, three tiers of arches in an oval amphitheater, seated 50,000

The Aurelian Wall—built in A.D. 272 to keep out the barbarians

---

Theater of Marcellus—finished in A.D. 13 and housed the great productions of Greek and Roman authors

---

Circus Maximus—huge chariot race track, 600 x 200 yards (549 km x 183 km), begun about 300 B.C., could seat 250,000

Baths of Caracalla—public baths built during the reign of Emperor Caracalla, A.D. 211–217

Hadrian's Arch—triumphal arch built during the reign of Emperor Hadrian, A.D. 117-138

Arch of Constantine—triumphal arch built during the reign of the Emperor Constantine, A.D. 324–337

Appian Way—ancient Roman highway begun in 312 B.C.

Emperor's Palace—beginning in A.D. 85, emperors lived here surrounded by an army of servants and officials

---

Monumental Math *(cont.)*

1. Which seated more people, the Colosseum or the Circus Maximus? How many more people?

   _____

2. Which triumphal arch is older, Constantine's or Hadrian's? Approximately how many years older? _____

3. The Pantheon is reputed to be one of the most beautiful domed buildings in the world. How long was it a temple to all gods before it became a Christian church? _____

4. When was the Emperor's Palace 1,900 years old? _____

5. The Appian Way was built to let people travel to Rome. The Aurelian Wall was built to keep some people out. How many years passed between the construction of these two Roman projects?

   _____

6. The Emperor's Palace was a place for emperors to live; the Castel Sant' Angelo was a place for emperors to be buried. Which was built first? How many years passed from the construction of one to the construction of the other? _____

7. Chariot races were popular in Rome for a long time. Approximately how much older is the Circus Maximus than the Theater of Marcellus?_____

8. Approximately how tall is Trajan's Column? _____

Building Arches in Rome

Look at a picture of the Colosseum still standing in Rome today. It is replete with archways. The same is true of Hadrian's Arch and some of the long bridge aqueducts. The arches have proved sturdy and lasted a long time.

Arches carry weight at the same time they allow for a door, a window, or a parade march passageway. The curved line at the top makes an interesting decoration.

In the space below, design your own building with one or more arches. It could be a giant arch on the streets of Rome for you, as emperor, to march under with your victorious troops. Inscribe a message on it to commemorate your triumph over the enemies of Rome. Other possibilities: draw a house or aqueduct with arches. Use encyclopedias and other reference books to get ideas.

Ancient, Medieval, and Modern

Most of us have heard someone say "That's ancient history" when they are talking about something that happened only a few days ago. They exaggerate to make the point that whatever is ancient history no longer matters for today. Is this really true?

Many important things we live with today started a long time ago. Historians divide history into the following categories:

Ancient (4000 B.C.—A.D. 500)

Medieval (A.D. 500—A.D. 1500)

Modern (1500—Present)

Place each of the events listed below in its time division by putting an A (Ancient), M (Medieval), or Mo (Modern) in the blank beside it.

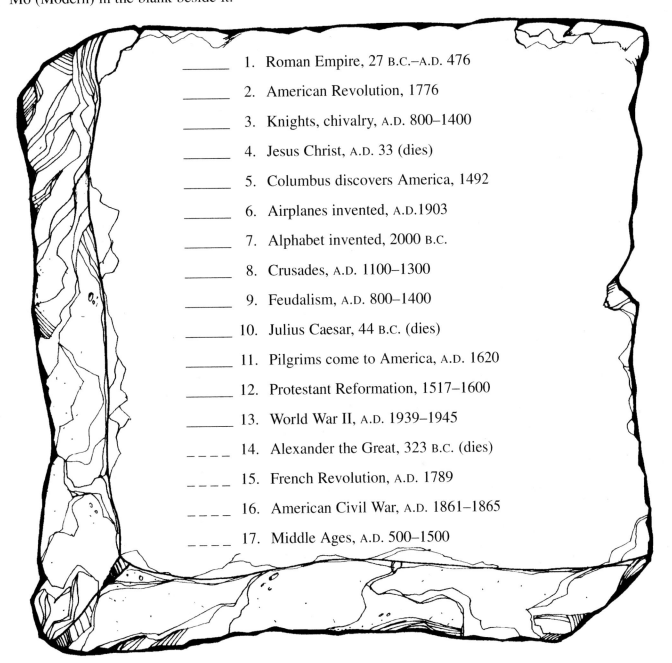

_____ 1. Roman Empire, 27 B.C.–A.D. 476

_____ 2. American Revolution, 1776

_____ 3. Knights, chivalry, A.D. 800–1400

_____ 4. Jesus Christ, A.D. 33 (dies)

_____ 5. Columbus discovers America, 1492

_____ 6. Airplanes invented, A.D.1903

_____ 7. Alphabet invented, 2000 B.C.

_____ 8. Crusades, A.D. 1100–1300

_____ 9. Feudalism, A.D. 800–1400

_____ 10. Julius Caesar, 44 B.C. (dies)

_____ 11. Pilgrims come to America, A.D. 1620

_____ 12. Protestant Reformation, 1517–1600

_____ 13. World War II, A.D. 1939–1945

_____ 14. Alexander the Great, 323 B.C. (dies)

_____ 15. French Revolution, A.D. 1789

_____ 16. American Civil War, A.D. 1861–1865

_____ 17. Middle Ages, A.D. 500–1500

Make a Calendar

The Romans gave us the names of months on our 12-month calendar. Can you match the month to its Roman origin?

_____ **1.** January	**a.** Maius
_____ **2.** February	**b.** Augustus, first emperor
_____ **3.** March	**c.** Seventh month—early calendar
_____ **4.** April	**d.** Purification festival—Februarius
_____ **5.** May	**e.** Janus, god of beginnings
_____ **6.** June	**f.** Aprilis
_____ **7.** July	**g.** tenth month, early calendar
_____ **8.** August	**h.** Julius Caesar's birthday month
_____ **9.** September	**i.** Oct—eighth month, early calendar
_____ **10.** October	**j.** Junius gens
_____ **11.** November	**k.** Ninth month, old calendar
_____ **12.** December	**l.** Mars

Group Project

Work in groups to create a calendar for the school year, showing important dates. Rulers, pencils, construction paper, and crayons will help. Each group may be assigned one or more months. The construction paper and basic format need to be close to identical in order for the calendar to be compiled and tied together with yarn.

The same prefixes that were used in some Latin calendar names are used for some geometric shapes. For example, an *octagon* has eight sides. How many sides does a *decagon* have? A *nonagon*? Draw and label these and other shapes on the opposite side of this paper.

Growing an Empire: Rome and America

Rome wasn't built in a day. This statement is true of the Roman empire as a whole which only gradually came under the authority of the city-state over six centuries. On the map below are the provinces of Rome and the dates when they came under her control.

Now look at the map of the United States on page 60. Like Rome, the pieces of the American "empire" were added gradually. Some territories did not become states until 1958.

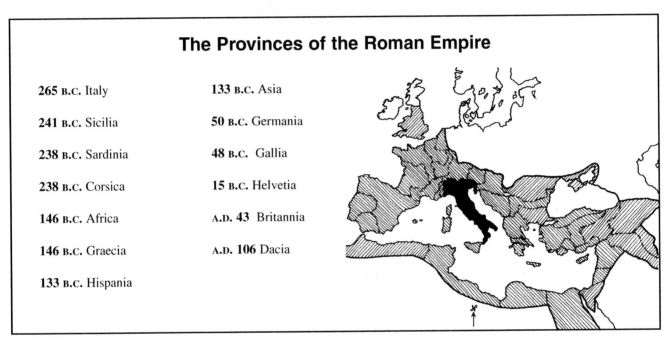

The Provinces of the Roman Empire

265 B.C. Italy	**133 B.C.** Asia
241 B.C. Sicilia	**50 B.C.** Germania
238 B.C. Sardinia	**48 B.C.** Gallia
238 B.C. Corsica	**15 B.C.** Helvetia
146 B.C. Africa	**A.D. 43** Britannia
146 B.C. Graecia	**A.D. 106** Dacia
133 B.C. Hispania	

Now use these maps and other references to compare the two world powers by answering the following questions.

1. How long did it take Rome to expand to its maximum size? _____
   The U.S.A. to expand to its current size? _____

2. In what geographical directions did Rome expand?_____
   In which geographical direction did the U.S.A. expand?_____

3. How many provincial divisions were added to the Roman Empire? _____
   How many states were added to the U.S.A. since the original states? _____
   How many states were added between 1791 and 1822? _____

4. What sea was important for Rome's expansion? _____
   What ocean was important for American expansion? _____

5. Rome gained independence from the Etruscan king of 50 B.C. From what power did the United States gain independence? _____

6. Rome subdued Germanic tribes, Gauls, Greeks, Asians, Carthagenians, and Jews in the course of her expansion. What other countries claimed land west of the unorganized territories of the early 1800s? _____

Growing an Empire: Rome and America *(cont.)*

Directions: Use the map below with the activity on page 59.

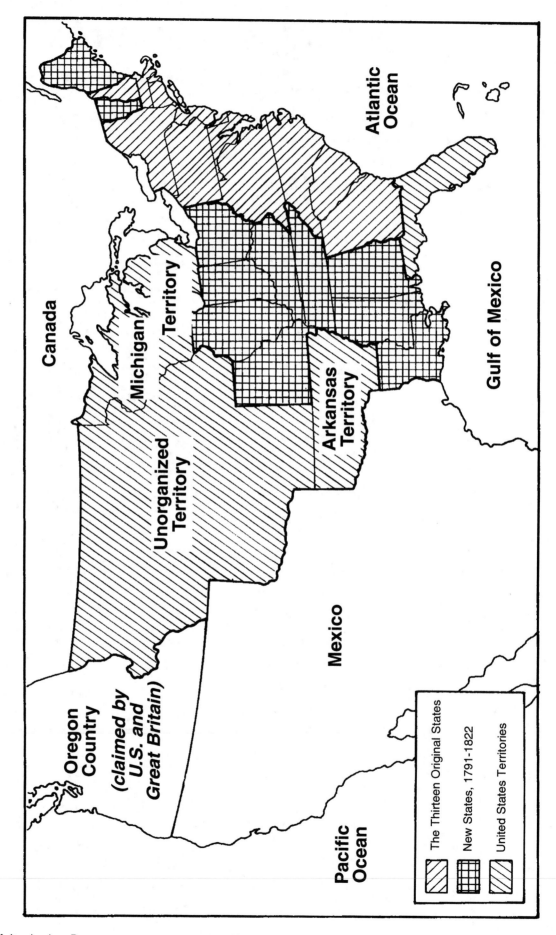

Atlantic Ocean

Canada

Michigan Territory

Unorganized Territory

Arkansas Territory

Gulf of Mexico

Mexico

Oregon Country

(claimed by U.S. and Great Britain)

Pacific Ocean

The Thirteen Original States

New States, 1791-1822

United States Territories

Roman Art

Romans were practical people and preferred realism in their art. They decorated their public buildings and homes with a variety of techniques, including mosaics, frescoes, and carvings.

Mosaics

The Romans decorated their homes and other buildings with mosaics, pictures made from tiny pieces of stone or tile set in clay. Some mosaics showed scenes from mythology or daily life, and others were abstract designs. You can make your own mosaic.

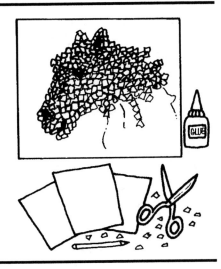

Materials: large piece of paper, assorted colored paper, foil (optional), pencil, scissors, glue

Directions: Sketch the design for your picture. Refer to James or another source for ideas, if you wish. Work on one section of your design at a time. Cut the colored paper into ¹/₂" (1.25 cm) squares and triangles. Fit the pieces together to cover the design area and glue them in place. If you wish, silver or gold foil can be used as an accent in your mosaic.

Frescoes

Another type of decoration was called a fresco. Frescoes are usually large murals made by painting on a building material, either clay or plaster, while it is still wet. When the wall dries, the design is permanent.

Materials: cardboard or poster board for base, plaster of Paris, blunt pencil, thinned paint, brushes

Directions: Spread an even coat of plaster of Paris on the base. Working quickly, use the blunt pencil to scratch a design on the plaster. While the plaster is wet, paint the design. Allow the plaster to dry naturally.

Carving

Romans worked in stone, ivory, and other materials to create statues and relief figures. You can achieve a similar effect with clay.

Materials: cardboard or poster board for base, self-hardening clay, blunt pencil, paint (optional)

Directions: Select a subject—a soldier, god, emperor, or scene from daily life. Use part of the clay to make a smooth layer on the cardboard. Shape small pieces of clay for each detail in the picture and press them onto the base. If desired, paint the clay while it is still wet or leave it plain. Allow your scuplture to air dry.

Comedy and Tragedy

Roman actors wore masks when they performed in the open-air amphitheaters. Sometimes they performed comedies to make the audience laugh. Sometimes they performed tragedies to make the audience cry.

The smiling mask (comedy) and the sad mask (tragedy) have become the symbols of the theater in the modern world.

On the back of this paper, write a short comic or tragic play. It could be about an emperor, a soldier, or a hero of Rome. You might write a dialogue between patricians and plebeians as they struggle for power in the government. You can dramatize the assassination of Julius Caesar along with the famous line "Et tu, Brute!" (And you, Brutus!) that shows how a former friend can "stab you in the back."

Here is an example of an original dialogue:

Why Do We Need the 12 Tables?

Patrician: What is the problem, Plebian?

Plebian: There is no justice. You, Patrician, have one set of laws. I, a plebian, have another set of laws.

Patricians: So what? We were here in Rome first! We come from the old families. We make the rules.

Plebian: Oh, yeah? Well, maybe you have been making the rules too long! We need the same rules for everyone.

Patrician: How could you do that?

Plebian: We get 12 big metal tables and carve the laws on them. That way everyone will know

what the laws are and get the same treatment.

Patricians: Well, it might work. We are all Romans.

Plebian: And we all should be treated as Romans.

Extension: Use papier mâché to make a mask. Decorate it according to the character it represents, smiling for comedy and a sad face for tragedy.

Sing Me a Song

Can you sing in Latin? Here are some songs for your class to perform at a special Roman dinner party.

Mica, Mica, Parva Stella

Mica, Mica, parva stella:
Miror quaenam sis tam bella!
Super terra in caelo
Alba gemma splendido.
Mica, Mica, parva stella,
Miror quaenam sis tam bella!

Barcam Remiga

Barcam remiga
lente in aqua
Hilare, hilare, hilare, hilare
Somnium est vita.

Tres Caecae Mures

Mures tres, mures tres
caecae currunt, caecae currant
Sequuntu sponsom agriculae,
Ab ea abscissae aunt caudulae
est plenius nihil stulitiae
quam mures tres.

Twinkle, Twinkle Little Star

Twinkle, twinkle little star
How I wonder what you are!
Up above the world so high
Like a diamond in the sky.
Twinkle, twinkle, little star,
How I wonder what you are!

Row, Row, Row Your Boat

Row, row, row your boat
gently down the stream.
Merrily, merrily, merrily, merrily
Life is but a dream.

Three Blind Mice

Three blind mice, three blind mice,
See how they run, see how they run!
They all ran after the farmer's wife,
She cut off their tails with a carving knife;
Did you ever see such a sight in your life,
As three blind mice?

Latin Pronunciation

Classical (Roman) Latin uses the same letters as English except for w. The letters y and z are not used often. Every letter is pronounced, and there is only one pronunciation for each consonant. Vowels may be long or short, but the difference is how long it takes to say each one.

Vowels

a as in father: trans

e as in they: me

i as in ski: si

o as in note: non

u as in rule: tu

Diphthongs

ae as in aisle: aes-tas

au as in ouch: au-tem

oe as in oil: coe-pi

Consonants: Most consonants have the same sound as in English, but c, g, and t are always hard.

c as in cat: ca-sa

g as in get: gens

t as in tin: tamen

v is pronounced as w, as in wine: vi-num

qu is a single sound, pronounced kw as in queen: e-quus

b before s or t has the sound of p

Let's Go to the Movies!

Ancient Rome was featured in many American movies during the 1950s and 1960s. Look at the examples to the right.

Make your own movie. Use a video camera to film your classmates in homemade togas. Have one of them play Mark Antony in Shakespeare's *Julius Caesar* and read the funeral oration at Caesar's funeral. One of the more "dramatic" students in the class should speak these famous lines: "Friends, Romans, countrymen, lend me your ears . . ." with a flair. Others in the crowd can react to what he says with well-timed "Oohs" and "Nos." Pick a student with steady hands or use a tripod to hold the camera and make your own movie about Rome.

Here are some jobs for your movie crew:

- **actors**

  Mark Antony, crowd

- **script preparer**

  photocopy section of *Julius Caesar*

- **costume preparer**

- **makeup**

- **sound effects**

- **film editor**

- **photographer**

- **set designer**

  coffin, column (cardboard)

- **director**

  the "boss"

- **lighting**

  work with photographer

- **cue card holder**

Ben Hur—Charleton Heston stars as a Jewish leader during the time of Jesus. This film features the most action-packed chariot race ever filmed.

Cleopatra—Elizabeth Taylor stars as the Egyptian queen who charms would-be Roman emperors.

Demetrius and the Gladiators—A gladiator becomes a Christian.

The Fall of the Roman Empire—Crazy emperors rule a lively Rome.

Julius Caesar—Marlon Brando stars in the Shakespearean play.

The Robe—The persecution of early Christians is portrayed.

Spartacus—Kirk Douglas plays a slave, a gladiator in training, who leads an almost successful slave revolt against Rome.

Quo Vadis—Rome and Christianity are featured.

Roman and American Coins

You may have seen someone in your neighborhood walking slowly and passing a long metal object back and forth over the ground. Chances are that person was looking for coins. The device the person was carrying was a metal detector that can tell you, without digging, that there is or is not a metal object beneath the surface of the ground. A coin collector waits for his metal detector to sound a beep before he starts digging.

Roman coins are still dug up today in parts of Europe. They can tell us a little bit about the emperors because they usually have a picture of one of the "Caesars" engraved on one side. The smallest "penny" coin of Rome was the *as*, followed by the *dupondius*, worth two *asses*, and the *sestertius*, worth four *asses*. A *denarius* was worth 16 *asses*, and the *aurea* could be exchanged for 100 *asses*.

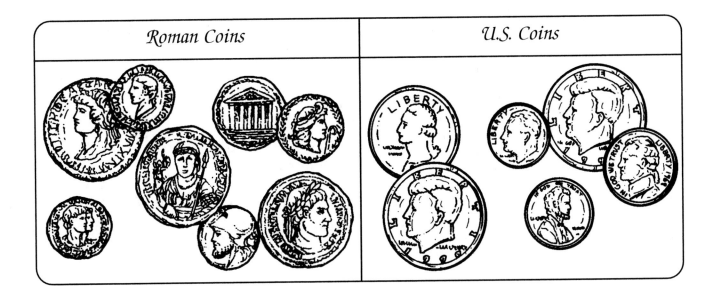

| *Roman Coins* | *U.S. Coins* |

Internet Extender

Write a summary explaining Roman coins and how they compare to the coins we use today.

Roman Coins
Search these key words or phrases: Byzantine Coins, Roman Coins

It is possible to view both sides of ancient coins and read information about their imprints. You can also learn about the manufactures, denominations and dating of old coins..

Design your own coin and then draw both sides of the coin in the circles.

Shopping with Roman Coins

2 asses = 1 dupondius	16 asses = 1 denarius
4 asses = 1 sestertius	100 asses = 1 aureau

1. You and your friend Claudius go shopping at the forum. You see a new toga on sale for five denarii, but all you are carrying is sestertii. How many sestertii will you need to pay for the toga? _____

2. You sample some Italian wine and purchase an amphorae of it for your household for 15 sestertii. You pay a slave three asses to deliver it. What was the total cost for the wine, in asses? _____

3. A wheat shipment has just arrived and you buy three bags of wheat at three denarii per bag. What is the total cost in sesterci? _____

4. Olive oil is used frequently for cooking. You buy a large amphorae of olive oil for ten dupondi. A slave delivers it for two asses. What is the total price of the oil in asses? _____

5. You see a very intelligent Greek slave who can read and write and may be the perfect teacher for your sons. The owner of the slave will sell the tutor for two aurei and even throw in his small library of Greek classics. You have 80 sesterti left. Can you afford this educational bargain? _____

6. The slave eats quite a bit. Each week you purchase two denarii more of food. How much is this in sestercii? _____

7. The tax man visits and demands that you "render unto Caesar" 12 aurei. How many asses do you owe? _____

Tunic and Toga

A tunic is a garment like a shirt or gown worn by both sexes among the ancient Greeks and Romans. It is usually presented as a knee-length garment that hangs loosely over the shoulders. A toga is a loose outer garment worn by citizens of Rome when appearing in public during a time of peace.

It is possible to make a simple tunic that will fit smaller students by simply cutting head and arm holes in a pillow case. Try them out with shorter students to see if they extend to the knee. For taller students, cut two pieces of sheet large enough to cover the student from shoulders to knees. Sew the sides. Gather the top and pin it at the shoulder. Tie the waist with a sash. Knee-length tunics require less cloth than full-length togas and may be easier to make. They can add the costume factor to any dramatic activity in the Rome unit.

Toga

Tunic

A Comfortable House in the City

Fill in the blanks as you read the following passage.
(Refer to the Roman house on page 69 to find the names of rooms.)

You are a patrician, a wealthy Roman. You can afford to have a country estate as well as a comfortable house in the city. You like to have friends like Claudius come for dinner.

As you walk from the forum after a day of shopping with Claudius, you turn off the Via Appia on to a side street. You pass by the (1) _____ that are closed off from the main house and remind the shopkeepers who share the building with you that it is time for the monthly rent.

As you walk into your private entryway, the (2) _____ , you immediately notice the delicious smells coming from the
(3) _____ , a Roman kitchen. You and Claudius stroll into the open air reception area, the (4) _____ , where you are met by slaves who bring you refreshments. The new Greek slave you purchased has been shown his new room and has deposited his books in your growing (5) _____ . After noting that the
(6) _____ is full after last night's rain, you lead Claudius into your study, the (7) _____ , where you show him a copy of Homer's *Odyssey* that the new slave brought with him.

After reading a few interesting passages, you lead Claudius out to the patio, or (8) _____ , then back inside where you settle down to eat in the dining room, the (9) _____ . After eating and a little musical entertainment, you offer to let Claudius stay the night your spare (10) _____ . You enjoy the luxurious living in your house, your (11) _____ .

Extension: Refer to the cutaway plan. Then, draw one or more rooms in detail. Show how you would decorate it and what your furniture would look like.

A Comfortable House in the City *(cont.)*

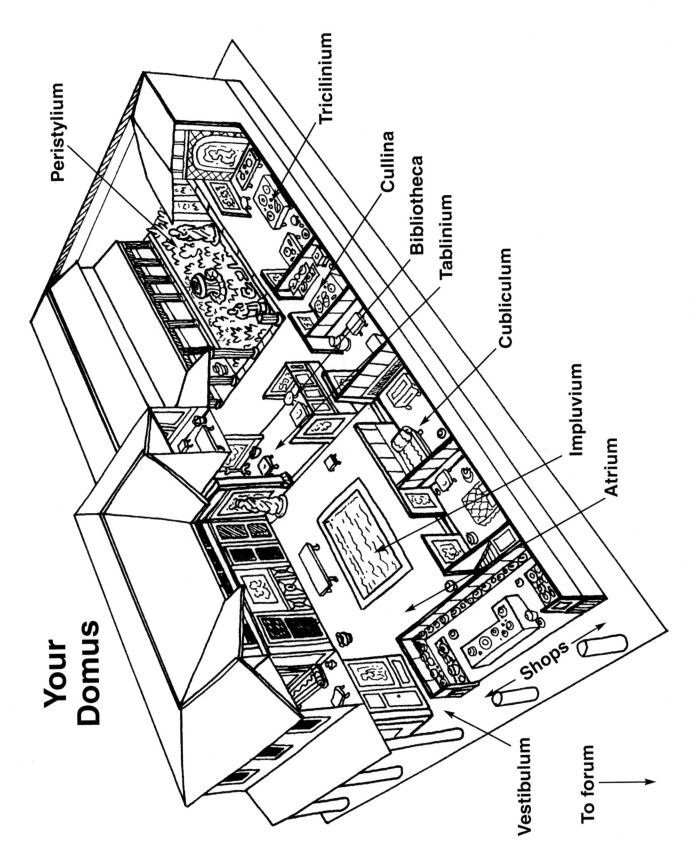

Peristylium

Tricilinium

Cullina

Bibliotheca

Tablinium

Cubiculum

Impluvium

Atrium

Your Domus

Shops

Vestibulum

To forum

Time Travelers

Internet Extender

Virtual Tour of Ancient Rome
Search these key words or phrases: Forum Romanum, Roman Forum

Activity Summary: Locate a Web site that will allow you to view the ruins of the ancient Roman Forum. If possible, share your results on a large monitor so that many students can participate in this interactive experience.

Directions:

1. Look at the photo of the Forum. Study it for a few minutes to see how splendid this area must have once been. Only the ruins remain today. You may see some modern buildings in the background; look for two statues on the top of the buildings. It is difficult to look at the ruins and tell what they once were. Move the cursor over the photo. You may be bale to click on the cursor to see specific buildings close up.

To learn more, search the phrase: Ancient Roman Forum.
Assignment: Make a list of the buildings that have been identified in the ruins and write a brief summary explaining the purpose or use of the three of them.

Culminating Activity: Prepare a printout of some of the Forum and related pictures for a bulletin board display.

• Print color copies of the entire Forum picture and close ups of the related buildings. Place the Forum in the center of your bulletin board, surrounded by the buildings and a written summary explanation of each one. Link the pictures with string of their locations in the Forum photo.

Extension: You may prepare a similar bulletin board featuring buildings and points of interest throughout the city of Rome by searching these key words and phrases: Ancient Rome: Images and Pictures, Virtual Tour of Ancient Rome, or Ancient Rome Visual Tour

Technology Extenders

The following activities may be used as conventional culminating projects or as technology extenders to reinforce the content learning of this unit with computer experience. Each activity is designed to involve the student in the merging of technology and the subject matter of this thematic unit.

1. Friends, Romans, and Countrymen

Software: any word processing program, such as Word, Word Perfect, etc.

Activity: Have students assume the role of one class of Roman society (e.g., *slave, plebeian, gladiator, patrician, soldier*) and then write journal entries about what elements of their lives need to be changed and what elements please them. Use special fonts, borders, etc., and save each entry to print as a booklet when the unit is over.

2. All Roads Lead to Rome

Software: any paint, draw, and graphics program

Activity: Using the map on page 72, give unlabeled copies to students and help them to scan it into their computers and then use the paint and draw program to color, enlarge, and label buildings, streets, and roads with appropriate fonts. Save, print, and post these finished products on the bulletin board.

3. Hail the Conquerors

Software: any database program contained in a software suite (*Works for Windows, ClarisWorks*, etc.)

Activity: After researching data, battles, and wars of ancient Rome, create a database with this information and help studens learn to use the computer to organize the elements in alphabetical and/or chronological order—i.e., Rome Conquers Italy: 200 B.C., Rome Defeats Hannibal: 219–201 B.C., Rome Conquers Greece: 146 B.C. , etc.

4. The Empires Strike Back

Software: any spreadsheet program

Activity: Research and discuss the concept of "empire" and help students create a spreadsheet to record basic characteristics of five or six empires (Roman, Babylonian, Spanish, Portuguese, British, Japanese). For each, record information in the following cells: *Time/Dates, Method* (war?), *Government* (republic?), *Influence* (language, law, etc.). Show students how these spreadsheets can be converted into graphs, saved, printed, and posted on the bulletin board.

5. Hannibal and the Elepahnts

Software: any desktop publishing program (*The Print Shop, Publisher*, etc.,)

Activity: After researching Hannibal's invasion over the Alps, help students use the computer to design a newspaper front page, composing such articles and headlines as "Beasts in the Streets," "Interview with Hannibal," "Feeding and Caring for Elephants," "Winter Warfare—Altitude, Attitude, and Alps."

6. Roman Inventions

Software: any multimedia program, such as *HyperStudio*, etc.

Activity: Group students and help them to prepare "slide show" presentations, containing narration, text, color, graphics, and sound on such Roman developments as *concrete, indoor plumbing and baths, roads, arches, aqueducts, walls*, and even *hair curling*. The multimedia report may incorporate photographs, diagrams, drawings, and other modern source material that illustrates these ancient cultural accomplishments.

Rome

Directions: Use the map below with the activity on page 71.

Via Appia Nuova

Caracalla

Colosseum

Arch of Constantine

Palatine Hills

Terme

Monte Capitoline

Forum

Baths of Caracalla

Viale Aventino

Via Del Corso

Mausoleum of Augustus

Cavour Bridge

Pantheon

Corso Vittorio

Tiber River

Palace of Justice

Castel St. Angelo

St. Peter's Square

Via delle Fornaci

Viale di Trastevere

Garibaldi Monument

Vatican City St. Peter's

Who Will Be Emperor? Game

OMEN

OMEN

Born to a patrician family, you may be in line to be the next leader of the Roman Empire.

START

OMEN

Who Will Be Emperor? Game *(cont.)*

OMEN

OMEN

OMEN

Will you make it? Or will one of your many rivals outmaneuver you to gain the imperial palace?

Omen Cards

YOU WIN A MAJOR BATTLE AGAINST BARBARIAN TRIBES. + 5 spaces	**YOU ARE TEMPTED BY AN EASTERN RULER AND IGNORE YOUR DUTIES.** - 5 spaces
THE CURRENT EMPEROR APPOINTS YOU GOVERNOR OF GAUL. + 3 spaces	**YOU LEAD AN ARMY INTO ROME AND TAKE CONTROL.** + 10 spaces
YOU LOSE A MAJOR BATTLE IN A CIVIL WAR FOR CONTROL OF THE EMPIRE. - 10 spaces	**YOU PARADE YOUR ARMY IN TRIUMPH THROUGH ROME.** + 7 spaces
THE CURRENT EMPEROR ADOPTS YOU AND TELLS OTHERS YOU ARE IN LINE FOR LEADERSHIP. + 10 spaces	**YOU ARE ACCUSED OF THEFT OF PUBLIC FUNDS.** - 7 spaces
YOU JOIN A 3-PERSON GOVERNMENT SHARING POWER IN THE EMPIRE. + 5 spaces	**THE SENATE VOTES YOU DICTATOR FOR LIFE.** + 15 spaces
YOU SUFFER A MINOR DEFEAT IN A FRONTIER BATTLE. - 5 spaces	**YOU ARE ELECTED TRIBUNE.** + 5 spaces
YOU ARE PROMOTED TO CONSUL AND MADE GENERAL OF A MAJOR ARMY. + 8 spaces	**YOUR RIVAL FOR THE CROWN SEIZES THE CITY OF ROME.** - 15 spaces
YOU ARE SEVERELY WOUNDED IN BATTLE AND LOSE YOUR AMBITION TO RULE ROME. - 15 spaces	**SEVERAL SENATORS DENOUNCE YOU PUBLICLY.** - 7 spaces
YOU CLEAR THE MEDITERRANEAN SEA OF PIRATES. + 10 spaces	**YOU GAIN NEW ALLIES IN THE SENATE.** + 5 spaces

Omen Cards *(cont.)*

FORMER ALLIES JOIN FORCES WITH YOUR RIVAL. - 5 spaces	**NEW PUBLIC BATHS YOU SPONSOR COLLAPSE, KILLING FOUR PEOPLE.** - 7 spaces
YOU NARROWLY ESCAPE AN ASSASSINATION ATTEMPT. - 10 spaces	**YOUR ALLIES ASSASSINATE A MAJOR RIVAL.** + 8 spaces
YOU SPONSOR GLADIATOR SHOWS IN THE COLOSSEUM. + 7 spaces	**THE COLOSSEUM SHOWS YOU SPONSOR ARE NOT A POPULAR SUCCESS.** - 5 spaces
YOU GO BROKE. - 10 spaces	**YOU INHERIT WEALTH.** + 11 spaces
A GOOD OMEN GREETS YOU ON THE MORNING OF A MAJOR BATTLE. + 4 spaces	**A BAD OMEN GREETS YOU ON THE MORNING OF A MAJOR BATTLE.** - 4 spaces
YOU PUBLISH A POPULAR BOOK, DETAILING YOUR MILITARY SUCCESS. + 9 spaces	**YOU BECOME WEALTHY FROM CONQUERING NEW PROVINCES.** + 4 spaces
YOU ARE DEPOSED AS TRIBUNE. - 5 spaces	**YOU BUILD A NEW FORUM, A POPULAR SHOPPING CENTER.** + 4 spaces
YOU ARE DEPOSED AS CONSUL. - 7 spaces	**YOU IGNORE RUMORS OF ASSASSINATION PLOTS.** - 6 spaces
YOU DEDICATE SEVERAL NEW PUBLIC WORKS WITH YOUR NAME ON THEM. + 8 spaces	**YOU ORGANIZE MORE EFFICIENT TAX COLLECTIONS.** + 3 spaces

Answer Key

Page 10

1. Latin language: answers will vary
2. Entertainment: plays, races, poetry readings, musical performances
3. Government/Politics: voting, senate, representatives (tribune), jury system
4. Architecture: concrete, aqueducts, wide roads, arches, bridges, temples, etc.
5. Religion: belief in afterlife, funeral, cremation or burial, etc.
6. Food: bread, wine, spicy foods, etc.
7. Housing: furniture, apartment buildings, plumbing, central heating, etc.
8. Clothing: sandals, socks, undergarments, jewelry, dyed and styled hair, wigs
9. Education: calendar, daily newspapers, Roman numerals, free public elementary school.
10. Arts and Crafts: cameos, mosaics, glass blowing, frescoes, etc.

Page 12

1. F
2. O
3. F
4. F
5. F
6. O
7. O
8. O
9. F
10. F
11. F
12. O
13. F
14. O

Page 15

1. 27 B.C.
2. 510/509 B.C.
3. A.D. 476
4. 1200 B.C.

5. A.D. 313
6. 753 B.C.
7. A.D. 33
8. A.D. 54–68
9. 264–241 B.C.
10. 218–201 B.C.
11. 146 B.C.
12. 50 B.C.
13. A.D. 6
14. 146 B.C.
15. 143 B.C.
16. 30 B.C.
17. 100–44 B.C.
18. 63 B.C.–A.D.14
19. 106–43 B.C.
20. 700s B.C.?
21. 400s B.C.–after 510 B.C.
22. 573 B.C.–716 B.C.
23. A.D. 272 – 337

Page 17

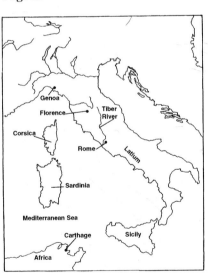

Page 18

1. Alba Longa
2. Romulus
3. Aeneas
4. Romulus and Remus survived an attempt to drown them as infants, and were suckled by a she-wolf.
5. Latins
6. 1184—753 = 431 years

Page 21

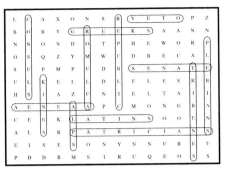

Page 23

1. republic; easier to have representatives than have all participate in decisions
2. U.S. government is more like Rome, representative government
3. No equality for all in Athens or Rome, although there was an attempt (Twelve Tables) to make laws more equal for citizens
4. Accept reasonable answers about equality and inequality in America.

Page 25 Elephants

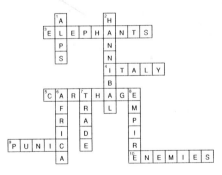

Page 29

1. victory
2. soldiers
3. prisoners
4. cheered
5. slave
6. crown
7. strangled
8. archway
9. inscribed

Answer Key *(cont.)*

Page 30

1. Christian
2. Barbarian
3. civil
4. Constantine
5. Constantinople
6. sacked
7. Byzantine
8. Catholic
9. Latin
10. Jesus Christ
11. The pope

Page 31

1. republic
2. Aeneas
3. Augustus
4. Brutus
5. empire
6. Cleopatra
7. Romulus
8. Julius Caesar
9. Cincinnatus
10. Tarquin
11. Remus
12. Nero
13. Horatio
14. Constantine
15. Mark Antony
16. Jesus
17. Hannibal

Page 32

1. Augustus
2. Rome
3. Herod
4. Cornelius
5. Caesarea
6. Pontius Pilate
7. denarius
8. Caesar's
9. crucify/crucifixion
10. Roman citizen

Page 40

1. 60; no
2. Augustus; Romulus Augustus

3. A.D. 284; A.D. 324.
4. Claudius; Galba
5. A.D. 161–180
6. 2;3
7. 367–69=298
8. after; before
9. 284–117=167

Page 42

(possible answers)

1. Augustus thumbs up—stability, rebuilt Rome
2. Caligula thumbs down—immoral, offended Jews
3. Claudius thumbs down—conquered Britain
4. Nero thumbs down—persecuted Christians
5. Tiberius thumbs up—good administration; thumbs down— suspicious, no entertainment
6. Aurelius thumbs up—honest administrator
7. Hadrian thumbs up—military leadership
8. Constantine thumbs up—stability

Page 43

1. b   9. b
2. e   10. e
3. d   11. c
4. c   12. a
5. a   13. e
6. c   14. b
7. d   15. d
8. a

Page 45

1. T
2. F
3. T
4. T
5. F
6. T
7. F
8. T
9. T
10. F

Essay: Accept all reasonable answers.

Page 47

1. C   5. E
2. F   6. A
3. G   7. B
4. H   8. D

Page 48

1. baths
2. gladiator
3. exercised
4. changing room
5. hot water
6. cold water
7. paterae
8. strigils
9. oliv oil

Page 49

1. Hera
2. Aphrodite
3. Venus
4. Minerva
5. handicrafts, wisdom
6. Bacchus
7. Neptune
8. Hades
9. Sol
10. Ares
11. hunting

1. Christian beliefs prevented them from sacrificing to the Roman gods, and so they were thought to be dangerous unbelievers who imperiled Rome by offending the gods.
2. polytheism: belief in many gods. It applies to the ancient Roman religion.
3. monotheism: belief in one God.— Judaism, Christianity, and Islam are monotheistic.

Page 50

1. Follow the local customs or traditions—get along with the local people.
2. I won the war.
3. You betrayed me, you were my friend.

Answer Key *(cont.)*

4. The peace and protection brought about by Roman armies throughout the empire
5. He did not do what needed to be done in an emergency; ignored his responsibility.
6. Do it today, do it now!
7. It takes time to build great things.
8. Rome was the center of civilization.

Page 51

Law

1. actually
2. authentic
3. according to law
4. a writ issued to bring a person before a judge
5. existing condition
6. obvious
7. advantage which determines value
8. retroactive
9. accused does not admit guilt and offers no defense to charges
10. for public good

Medicine

1. loss of feeling
2. heart
3. skin
4. hearing
5. children's health
6. nervous system
7. bones
8. x-ray images
9. urinary tract
10. old age

Music

1. low female voice
2. soft
3. loud
4. highest adult male voice
5. highest woman's or boy's voice

Other

1. equal exchange
2. free
3. and so forth
4. unwelcome individual
5. equally to each person

Page 52

1. deject
2. subscribe
3. inspect
4. remit
5. progress
6. compel
7. transfer
8. conduct
9. interdict

Page 53

1. XXIII
2. CLXXII
3. LXXVIII
4. DCCCLXXVI
5. XXXIX
6. CDVII
7. 25
8. 113
9. 251
10. 370
11. XXXVI
12. CCXXV
13. CLXII
14. XCVII
15. C
16. LX

Page 55

1. Circus Maximus: 200,000
2. Hadrian's arch: 199 years

3. 485 years
4. 1985
5. 584 years
6. Emperor's Palace: 51 years
7. 313 years
8. 97' (29.6 m)

Page 57

1. A
2. Mo
3. M
4. A
5. M
6. Mo
7. A
8. M
9. M
10. A
11. Mo
12. Mo
13. Mo
14. A
15. Mo
16. Mo
17. M

Page 58

1. e
2. d
3. l
4. f
5. a
6. j
7. h
8. b
9. c
10. i
11. k
12. g

decagon-10 nonagon-9

Page 59

1. Rome: 600+ years. U.S.A.: less than 200 years

2. Rome: North, South, East, West; U.S.A.: West, South
3. Rome: 41, U.S.A.: 37, 11
4. Rome: Mediterranean U.S.A.: Pacific Ocean
5. England
6. Mexico, Great Britain

Page 65

1. made of metal, leader's face done in profile, different values, round, lettering inscribed around the edges
2. e pluribus unum—out of many, one

Page 66

1. 20 sestertii
2. 63 asses
3. 36 sestertii
4. 22 asses
5. Yes (2 aurei = 200 asses; 80 sestertii = 320 asses)
6. 8 sestertii
7. 1200 asses

Page 68

1. shops
2. vestibulum
3. cullina
4. atrium
5. bibliotheca
6. impluvium
7. tablinium
8. peristylium
9. triclinium
10. cubiculum
11. domus

Bibliography

Nonfiction

The Bible. New International Version. (various sources)

Brandt, Keith. *Ancient Rome*. (Troll Associates, 1985)

Burrell, Roy. *The Romans*. (Oxford University Press, 1991)

Eyewitness Travel Guides: Rome. (Dorling Kindersley Publishing, Inc., 1999)

Gelinas, Paul J. *History of the World for Young Readers*. (Grossett and Dunlap, 1965)

Humphrey, Kathryn Long. *Pompeii: Nightmare at Midday*. (Houghton Mifflin, 1995)

James, Simon. *Ancient Rome*. (Alfred Knopf, 1990)

Macauley, David. *City*. (Houghton Mifflin, 1974)

Peris, Carme and Gloria and Oriol Verges. *The Greek and Roman Eras*. (Barrons, 1988)

Reid, T. R. "Rise and Fall of the Roman Empire," (*National Geographic*, July 1997)

———. "The World According to Rome," (*National Geographic*, August 1997)

Robinson, Charles Alexander, Jr. *The First Book of Ancient Rome*. (Franklin Watts, 1984)

Rutland, Jonathan. *See Inside a Roman Town*. (Franklin Watts, 1986)

Simkins, Michael. *Warriors of Rome*. (Blandford, 1990)

Tappan, Eva March. *The Story of the Roman People: An Elementary History of Rome*. (Riverside, 1938)

Fiction

Shakespeare, William. *Julius Caesar*. (various sources)

Activity Books

Jeffries, David. *Thematic Unit: Ancient Greece*. (Teacher Created Resources, Inc., 1993)

Sterling, Mary Ellen. *Thematic Unit: Ancient Egypt*. (Teacher Created Resources, Inc., 1992)

Audio Visual

Roman City School Kit. (PBS Video) Includes video modules and computer software.